ROBERT MUGABE'S LOST JEWEL OF AFRICA

'You have given me the Jewel of Africa.'

The words of Robert Mugabe to former Prime Minister Ian Smith in respect of Southern Rhodesia; it was uttered by him on 3 March 1980, a fortnight before that country achieved its independence under the new name of Zimbabwe.[1]

By the Same Author

By Swords Divided: Corfe Castle in the Civil War (Halsgrove, 2003)
Thomas Hardy: Christmas Carollings (Halsgrove, 2005)
Enid Blyton and her Enchantment with Dorset (Halsgrove, 2005)
Agatha Christie: The Finished Portrait (Tempus, 2007)
Tyneham: A Tribute (Halsgrove, 2007)
Mugabe: Teacher, Revolutionary, Tyrant (The History Press, 2008)
T. E. Lawrence: The Enigma Explained (The History Press, 2008)
The Story of George Loveless and the Tolpuddle Martyrs (Halsgrove, 2008)
Father of the Blind: A Portrait of Sir Arthur Pearson (The History Press, 2009)
Agatha Christie: The Pitkin Guide (Pitkin Publishing, 2009)
Jane Austen: An Unrequited Love (The History Press, 2009)
Arthur Conan Doyle: The Man behind Sherlock Holmes (The History Press, 2009)
HMS Hood: Pride of the Royal Navy (The History Press, 2009)
Purbeck Personalities (Halsgrove, 2009)
Bournemouth's Founders and Famous Visitors (The History Press, 2010)
Jane Austen: An Unrequited Love (The History Press, 2009)
Thomas Hardy: Behind the Mask (The History Press, 2011)
Hitler: Dictator or Puppet (Pen & Sword Books, 2011)
A Brummie Boy goes to War (Halsgrove, 2011)
Winston Churchill: Portrait of an Unquiet Mind (Pen & Sword Books, 2012)
Charles Darwin: Destroyer of Myths (Pen & Sword Books, 2013)
Beatrix Potter: Her Inner World (Pen & Sword Books, 2013)
T. E. Lawrence: Tormented Hero (Fonthill, 2014)
Agatha Christie: The Disappearing Novelist (Fonthill, 2014)
Lawrence of Arabia's Clouds Hill (Halsgrove, 2014)
Kindly Light: The Story of Blind Veterans UK (Fonthill, 2015)
Jane Austen: Love is Like a Rose (Fonthill, 2015)
Thomas Hardy at Max Gate: The Latter Years (Halsgrove, 2016)
Corfe Remebered (Halsgrove, 2017)
Thomas Hardy: Bockhampton and Beyond (Halsgrove, 2017)
Mugabe: Monarch of Blood and Tears (Austin Macauley, 2017)
Hitler's Insanity: A Conspiracy of Silence (Fonthill, 2018)
Making Sense of Marilyn (Fonthill, 2018)

ROBERT MUGABE'S LOST JEWEL OF AFRICA

ANDREW NORMAN

FONTHILL

Fonthill Media Language Policy

Fonthill Media publishes in the international English language market. One language edition is published worldwide. As there are minor differences in spelling and presentation, especially with regard to American English and British English, a policy is necessary to define which form of English to use. The Fonthill Policy is to use the form of English native to the author. Andrew Norman was born and educated in England and Southern Rhodesia; therefore British English has been adopted in this publication.

Fonthill Media Limited
Fonthill Media LLC
www.fonthillmedia.com
office@fonthillmedia.com

First published in the United Kingdom and the United States of America 2017

British Library Cataloguing in Publication Data:
A catalogue record for this book is available from the British Library

ISBN 978-1-78155-688-7

Typeset in 10pt on 13pst Sabon
Printed and bound in England

Foreword

Africa is a continent that can only be described by superlatives. It has the clearest skies, with both twinkling stars and shooting stars that fall to their deaths in the most spectacular way; the most magnificent and varied collection of wild animals; and the most exquisite flowering plants and trees. Into this somewhat surreal world in 1956, a thirteen-year-old white schoolboy from England is suddenly projected. As he familiarises himself with his new surroundings in his new, adoptive country of Southern Rhodesia, he can only stare in wonder.

His new home is a settlement called Thornhill, near Southern Rhodesia's third largest town of Gwelo, where his father, Christopher (or 'Chris'), has taken up a post as headmaster. Unbeknown to himself and his family, another schoolmaster, this time a black person, had lived and taught in Gwelo two years previously in 1954. His name was Robert Gabriel Mugabe, and he would one day become his country's leader.

Andrew explores, makes friends with both blacks and whites, becomes used to being called '*piccanin baas*' by the family's black houseboy/garden boy, Timot, and seamlessly adapts to the colonial way of life. Gradually, however, he becomes aware of tensions. The Afrikaners (who make up about half of the white population) constantly complain about the treatment meted out to them by the British in the Boer (South African) Wars of 1880–1881 and 1899–1902—this, despite the passage of over half a century. As for the black people, they grow increasingly frustrated as they see their legitimate attempts to gain freedom and independence being constantly thwarted by the whites.

Preface

This is the story of Southern Rhodesia, from the time of its earliest known inhabitants, the Bushmen, to their displacement by the Bantu; the invasion by the Matabele under King Mzilikazi; the advent of the white missionaries; and the arrival of Cecil Rhodes and his Pioneer Column of early settlers, up to independence in 1980. This is the romantic land of the high veld; of teeming game; of the great river Zambezi and the mighty Victoria Falls; and of enormous mineral wealth. This was the country that Robert Mugabe—its future leader—referred to as 'the Jewel of Africa'. Yet, in this land of plenty, tensions in the mid-twentieth century were mounting between its black inhabitants and the whites, including those of British and Afrikaner stock: tensions which would one day boil over into a civil war in which Southern Rhodesia's neighbours would also become involved.

Included is the story of the Boer War and the 'Great Trek' of Afrikaners northward from the Cape; of explorer and missionary David Livingstone, the first white man to see the Victoria Falls and who named them after his Queen; of Cecil Rhodes, who gave the country its name; of bloody battles between the British and the Matabele; of a hunter who was mauled by a lion and lived to tell the tale; of Great Zimbabwe and the fabled Zimbabwe ruins; of an interview with one of the early pioneers, Mrs Jeannie Boggie; and, finally, of Ian Smith and his Unilateral Declaration of Independence—'UDI'.

The author has first-hand knowledge of the country, having arrived there with his parents in 1956. He describes what it was like to arrive in a British colony in the last decades of the colonial era; the wonders of Wankie Game Reserve (now Hwange National Park); a schoolboy expedition to the Eastern Districts in search of the elusive 'stone door ruin'; and a personal friendship that developed between himself and his family's black servant, Timot, at a time of racial segregation.

CONTENTS

1
Childhood:
A Great Adventure Looms

The year is 1956, the place is Lichfield, Staffordshire, in the Midlands of England. Our home is the Beacon School, an establishment for those who, at this time, are termed educationally subnormal (ESN) boys, where my father is headmaster. My parents and my sister, Jane, and I live on the premises. I am in my bedroom looking at my stamp collection. I collect stamps from all over the world, but in my opinion, the most attractive are those of Britain and her Commonwealth of Nations.

I am aged thirteen and a pupil at the city's King Edward VI Grammar School. Meanwhile, my sister, Jane, who is three years younger, attends Christ Church Primary School, which entails a walk of a quarter of a mile or so across 'The Moggs' with its streams, woods, and meadows. The highlight of my life is receiving my weekly allowance of pocket money—the number of pennies being arrived at by multiplying my age in years by two—and I am currently saving up to purchase the guard's van for my Hornby Dublo gauge '00' electric train set. It costs the princely sum of 7 shillings and 9 pence, and I can see it through the toy shop window as I pass by twice a day on the way to and from school, where I pause to gaze at it covetously. Other pleasures are making catapults, swapping cigarette cards with my friends, and staging imaginary battles with my fort and lead soldiers. I also possess a modest collection of farm animals, also made of lead, as well as a 'Fordson Major' tractor, a dumper truck, and various other 'Dinky' toys, all of which I keep carefully wrapped in tissue paper when not in use. A memorable event for me was the 1956 FA Cup Final, which our neighbour's son, Michael (whose parents own the only television in the street), invited me to watch with him and his family. Newcastle United played Manchester City and won 3-1.

Memories of the Second World War were still fresh in the mind. At the edge of the Beacon School's playing fields, for example, was an enormous air-raid shelter, large enough to accommodate the entire population of staff and pupils. From my bedroom window, across the drive, was the vegetable garden, where in the holiday times I helped the Beacon School's gardener, Mr Asher, a retired Army sergeant-major. It was he who introduced me to the joys of cultivating antirrhinums and nasturtiums, and slipped me the occasional half a crown—a huge sum for me in those days. On the far side of the lower lawn was a chestnut tree, which had a particular significance. The previous headmaster of the Beacon School, Mr G. F. Taylor, had two sons and one of them had planted this tree when a boy. It had now grown to a height of 30 feet or so. Sadly, he was subsequently killed in early 1944 in Italy at the Battle of Monte Cassino. Finally, when my father took over the headship, he discovered in the headmaster's desk an Army service revolver, fully loaded. If 'The Hun' had succeeded in invading, Mr Taylor, who had fought in the Great War (1914–1918), would have been ready for him.

Each year, we had a fortnight's holiday; for example, at modest guest houses in Weymouth, Dorset, or Buckland Brewer in Devonshire, or at a caravan on the North Wales coast. However, none of us travelled far afield in those days, even when my father purchased his first car—a Standard 'Vanguard' model—which he used sparingly, and spent more time washing and polishing than driving. My mobility was somewhat improved, however, when I prevailed upon my father to buy me a spanking new 'Raleigh Super Lenton' bicycle with drop-handlebars. I was now able to cycle along the narrow Staffordshire lanes to nearby villages, and this gave me a great feeling of freedom and independence. These were the modest parameters of my world. Little did I dream that shortly, this situation was rapidly to change.

As far as academic school work was concerned, I was the despair of my parents, and the only truly happy times that I remember were those spent at primary school with my adored teacher Miss Harrison, who took us for 'nature walks' and always encouraged, but never scolded. Having arrived home from school each day, my ambition was to get the homework done as quickly as possible and then call on Michael for a game of 'knuckledibs' or 'cowboys and Indians'. As for real adventure, this was provided by a weekly magazine for boys called the *Eagle* (my sister had the *Girl*), which was delivered by the postman—each issue costing threepence. Every Friday, I rushed home from school, bursting with anticipation, desperate to savour every word of the *Eagle* during the forthcoming weekend. It was edited by a gentleman whose name rolled off the tongue: Mr Marcus Morris. Through its pages, one could travel to Arizona with cowboy Geoff Arnold in *Riders of the Range*, and come face to face with Red Indians, deserts and cacti, and great red mountains. One could even journey into space with *Dan Dare, Pilot of the Future*. The *Eagle* also contained many real-life stories, such as *Cortez, Conqueror of Mexico* and *Lincoln of America*. However, it was those stories that involved missionaries, such as Mary Slessor and Dr David Livingstone—who was also a great explorer—that fascinated me most. In fact, the only subjects that I had found in any way interesting at junior school were nature study and religious studies: in these, I always came top of the class! The biblical stories fascinated me, being as fresh and as real as they were almost 2,000 years ago. At Grammar School, even these pleasures were denied to me, and I found the syllabus tedious and uninspiring.

So here we were, the archetypal English, lower-middle-class family, living conventional lives, attending church regularly on Sundays, and in the afternoon going for 'a drive' in the Standard Vanguard.

My father was an avid newspaper reader, and listened to every available news bulletin on the wireless. However, I caught him out one day when King George V died (on 6 February 1952), and I was the first in the family to hear the sad news.

Life would undoubtedly continue in much the same way, and we had no reason to expect otherwise, until my father noticed an advertisement in the *Times Educational Supplement*. The advertisement was for the headship of a school, 'Glengarry', similar to the one in Lichfield, but catering for both boys and girls, part boarding and part day, in Gwelo, Southern Rhodesia.

To cut a long story short, he duly applied; travelled to London, to Rhodesia House (High Commission for Southern Rhodesia); was interviewed; and, to everyone's surprise, including his own, was duly appointed to the post. The contract also required that my mother, Jean, would be the school's matron—a position that she currently held here at the Beacon School.

We had a foretaste of Southern Rhodesia when my father established contact with the current headmaster of Glengarry School, Mr Bonniwell, to whom my mother and I (both keen philatelists) were extremely grateful on account of the wonderfully picturesque Rhodesian stamps that arrived periodically on the envelopes of his letters. I already had several such stamps in my collection, including a three-penny depicting King George V in blue, with the Victoria Falls in sepia. Could it really be that we would one day have the opportunity to see what was surely one of the wonders of the natural world? Another favourite of mine was inscribed: 'Rhodesia & Nyasaland 1855 1955 Livingstone 1/-'. It depicted David Livingstone's head and shoulders, with the Victoria Falls in the background in blue and purple. This was to commemorate the centenary of the great explorer's first sighting of Victoria Falls on 16 November 1855—he was the first European to do so.

Mr Bonniwell, in one of his letters, which bore the address that was shortly to become our own—'Glengarry School, P.O. Box 655, Gwelo, Southern Rhodesia'— described how, from his office window, he had observed a pair of banded cobras writhing about on the lawn as he wrote. On a more practical level, he advised us to purchase special raincoats (trench coats), which he assured us would be a boon in the rainy season. They should be of the best quality and rubber-lined. We should also bring with us some thick blankets, to protect us from the cold in the Rhodesian winter (which started around the month of July, and lasted for about six weeks).

'Norman will now address the class for 10 minutes on the subject of Southern Rhodesia,' announced my teacher, Mr Cooper, who had got wind of the fact that my family was shortly to relocate to that country. I stood up and faced my fellow schoolboys. There was an air of unreality about the proceedings. Was it true that we were really going to a landlocked country in the heart of Africa, one which until then was, for us, simply a place marked in red on the map—as was much of the world at that time, it being under British sovereignty? Nervously, I reeled off the required statistics.

Southern Rhodesia is a country of some 150,000 square miles in surface area, or roughly 1.6 times larger than the United Kingdom. It contains 180,000 or so people of European origin, 2.3 million Africans, and 13,000 other races. In other words, for every white person, there are thirteen black people. The country is bordered by two rivers—the Zambesi to the north and the Limpopo to the south. Southern Rhodesia is part of a federation that includes Northern Rhodesia and Nyasaland. The average height of the land is 4,700 feet above sea level, which is 1,500 feet higher than England's highest mountain, Scafell Pike in the Lake District. So much for the dry statistics. The true reality, to which no book or manual, however descriptive, could ever do justice, would soon be upon us.

2

The Adventure Begins

A removal company in Lichfield packed our belongings into fourteen wooden crates, each of which was almost as tall as I was, with a lining of heavy foil to protect its contents during the forthcoming long sea voyage. Once packed, the crates were reinforced with battens, then bound around with metal ribbons.

My mother insisted on taking her sturdy 'Singer' hand sewing machine with her, for which a crate with a slot-in lid had to be specially made. Finally, we sent 'change-of-address' cards to all our friends. When the great day arrived, Mr Eric Earl, my father's deputy head, drove us from Lichfield to Southampton, calling in at Winchester on the way, where we said goodbye to my great-grandmother, Jane Benwell, with whom I entrusted my most treasured possession: the Hornby Dublo electric train set—all my other toys, sadly, had been disposed of. She had given it to me as a present three years previously on my tenth birthday.

As we drove through Southampton, we were all shocked to see so many bombed-out buildings, and I recalled my parents telling me how, from Winchester, where they had once lived, they had seen during the recent world war a red glow in the night sky after a German wartime raid, as the city burned and British fighter aircraft engaged in dogfights with the enemy.

The great ship *Edinburgh Castle*, on which we were to travel, with its distinctive, lilac-painted hull, white superstructure, and single red and black funnel—the traditional livery of the Union Castle Line—towered above the docks. Built by Harland & Wolff of Belfast, and launched on 16 October 1947 by HRH Princess Margaret, she was the third of the company's ships to bear that name. She weighed in at 28,705 tonnes, was 747 feet in length, and had an 84-foot beam. She could achieve a top speed of 22½ knots. In 1954, she had broken the speed record for the voyage from Southampton to the Cape of Good Hope, with a time of eleven days and twenty-one hours. Like her sister ship, *Pretoria Castle II*, she could carry 227 first-class and 478 cabin-class passengers.

Having crossed from shore to ship via the gangplank, which was an adventure in itself, our first port of call was the Purser's Office, where we would be allocated our cabins (we travelled cabin class, which was in between first class and tourist class). The arrangement was that my mother and father would share one cabin and Jane and I another.

Hanging on the wall of the office was a print of a medieval building with masses of blue wisteria growing on its ancient wall. Mother recognised it at once. It was Cheyney Court in Winchester: a city in which she had spent much of her childhood and youth, and which was, therefore, very dear to her heart. Showing great temerity, she asked the Purser if she could have it. He agreed. So, the picture went to Southern Rhodesia with us, and it made her homesick every time she looked at it.

Finally, on Thursday 19 April 1956, we set sail on the fourteen-day voyage to Cape Town for what was to be the adventure of our lives.

At mealtimes, we children sat at a separate table from the grown-ups. To be given a menu, beautifully illustrated with scenes of Africa, and to be asked to choose from it, was a novelty. As for the food, it was a revelation, compared with what was available under the austere conditions of post-war Britain. At breakfast, for example, there were seven courses to choose from, and several choices available for each course.

Spain's Cape Finisterre (meaning literally 'the end of land'), which came into view before gradually disappearing in the mist, was the last we saw of continental Europe. We had been warned that the Bay of Biscay might be rough, but in the event it was glassy-smooth. There was, however, a considerable swell. No one had warned us that great ships make incredible creaking and straining noises as they plough through mighty oceans, and sometimes it seemed as if the *Edinburgh Castle* would never right herself as she leaned over more and more until the creaking finally stopped and she commenced to lean the opposite way.

At Las Palmas—where we saw palm trees for the first time—we disembarked briefly. Jane purchased a Spanish doll with her pocket money, and I haggled, successfully, over the price of a 'genuine' Parker fountain pen, only to discover that I had left the wallet containing my pocket money in my cabin on the ship. A local man sidled up to my father and whispered in his ear, 'You like dirty postcards?' at which my father first recoiled in shock before composing himself and quipping jokingly, 'Later, later!' The voyage continued.

My father, never a one for practicalities, mistook a small ventilator in the cabin for an ashtray and when, having filled it with cigarette butts and the ash from his pipe, he inadvertently switched it on, it blew its contents straight back into his face.

As we travelled southwards, it became very hot, and my mother began to suffer terribly with swollen feet. She therefore took care, when venturing out onto the sun deck, to keep in the shade. Beef tea was recommended for mid-morning to replace the salt lost from the body in perspiration. A distinguished fellow traveller was J. Alan Cash, the well-known photographer from London, who often had photographs published in *Country Life* and other prestigious magazines. He and his wife promised to come and visit us in Rhodesia (and sure enough, they kept their word).

There was much hilarity when we 'Crossed the Line'—the Equator. 'King Neptune' and his Court duly tried and sentenced many 'miscreants', all of whom were unceremoniously ducked in the swimming pool. There was also a fancy-dress party, and races were organised in which Jane won an oil-painting set and I a 'Riley' Dinky car, which I was delighted with as it would normally have cost me more than a week's pocket money. To mark the occasion, we were each presented with a special scroll on which was depicted Neptune, a map of the world, Britannia (a seated female figure with trident and helmet, representing Britain), and a lion. When Jane and I said we thought we had seen a shark, the sailors vigorously denied it. They were superstitious, and for them, this would have been a bad omen.

My father loved poetry and was in the habit of reading it aloud to my sister and me. A favourite was *The Rime of the Ancient Mariner* by Samuel Taylor Coleridge, featuring an albatross. There was excitement on deck one day when not one, but two of these magnificent but mysterious birds, whose wingspan is in the order of 10 feet, were seen gliding effortlessly a few hundred yards astern, presumably riding on the thermals produced by the hot gases emanating from the funnel. They followed us for several days, and then were gone.

Our journey was almost at an end, but first there was a problem to be negotiated: the notorious 'Cape Rollers' (turbulent seas arising where the waters of the Atlantic and Indian Oceans meet). Everyone was seasick, except for a very few, including my mother, who appeared, as usual, for her evening dinner as if to say, 'What is all the fuss about?'

Finally, early on the morning of 2 May 1956, when it was still dark, my parents roused Jane and me from sleep and dragged us, bleary-eyed, from our cabin and up onto the deck. What excitement as we saw the lights of Cape Town and Table Mountain looming over the city.

As the ship made its approach, we passed Robben Island, situated 6 miles out to sea in Table Bay (its name deriving from the Dutch '*robben*', meaning a seal—creatures that abounded in great numbers in the waters hereabouts). In this very year, 1956, Nelson Rolihlahla Mandela, lawyer, political leader, and member of the African National Congress (ANC), was charged with high treason but acquitted. However, before long, he and Robben Island would become all too well acquainted.

3

Another Continent: Virtually Another World

Having disembarked from the ship and passed through Customs and Immigration without any problems, we had a day to spare before our train departed; so we took a taxi into Cape Town where we saw black people for the very first time in our lives. This was South Africa's oldest city: founded by Jan van Riebeeck on 6 April 1652, when he established a fort on behalf of the Dutch East India Company, together with a settlement on the shores of Table Bay at the foot of Table Mountain.

After lunch, we were met by two glamorous young female representatives from a well-known publishing firm (who were presumably hoping that when father took up his new post as headmaster, he would become their customer and purchase some of their books for his school). Before we knew it, they whisked us off in a gleaming Buick automobile to the district of Constantia, where there were several old-established vineyards (of which the oldest and most famous was Groot ('great') Constantia, established in 1684 by Governor Simon Van der Stel, and named after his wife). Here, the houses were 'Cape Dutch' in character, with high gables and shuttered windows. This style of architecture, based on the traditional designs of the Netherlands, was brought to South Africa by the early settlers from Holland. The settlers were originally known as 'Boers' (this being the Dutch word for 'farmer'). However, the 'Boers' were subsequently referred to as 'Afrikaners', and their language became known as 'Afrikaans'.

We did not quite reach the summit of Table Mountain because mother, always a nervous passenger, was terrified by the winding road and its adjacent precipices, and by the young lady driver, who talked incessantly and made wild gesticulations, exhorting us, as often as not with either one or no hands on the steering wheel, to admire the scenery. Mother, panic stricken, insisted that our hosts stopped halfway up Signal Hill. Nonetheless, we were fortunate enough to obtain magnificent and breathtaking views of the town below, and of the oceans: Atlantic to our right and Indian to our left. By now, Table Mountain was visible in all its glory: its famous tablecloth of cloud spilling over from its summit and quickly evaporating in the warmer air below. We were then taken to a tea shop where Jane and I, once again taking a rare opportunity to order exactly what we wished—just like grown-ups—ate fifteen scones between us.

In the late afternoon, carrying a large wicker basket given to us by the ladies, and containing exotic fruits such as grenadillas (passion fruits) and guavas—neither of which we had seen before—we boarded the train at Cape Town's station. We had a compartment to ourselves, but meals were taken in the dining car, where my father made the mistake of ladling spoonfuls of what he thought was brown sugar onto his water melon, only to find that it was ground ginger.

The journey north took four days and four nights, during which time we travelled for 200 miles through the great Karoo Desert: the arid brown landscape of which was dotted with scrub and seemed to go on for ever. At night, the stars were clearer than we had ever seen them, and every minute or two a shooting star would appear. From the guide book we learned that in prehistoric times this region was inhabited by Hottentots (the name 'Karoo' deriving from a Hottentot word meaning bare)—an aboriginal people of Mongolian appearance. Smallpox, introduced inadvertently by the early Europeans settlers, decimated their numbers and they were now virtually extinct in pure form, though some had interbred with other tribes. Rainfall here was 10 inches per year maximum. Later, away to the east, the jagged peaks of the Drakensberg Mountains came into view.

At Kimberley in the Northern Cape Province—as at every other railway station along the way—black men, women, and children, all barefoot, appeared as if from nowhere, and ran alongside the train until it stopped. Then, they thrust tiny baskets with lids, intricately woven from reeds, and animals exquisitely carved out of wood of various colours, through the open windows, crying '*tickie, baas*', '*tickie, baas*' (a '*tickie*', as a fellow-traveller explained to us, being a threepenny piece). The black womenfolk carried their infants—'*piccanins*'—on their backs in tightly wrapped shawls. Some balanced pots, or other items (such as a sewing machine similar to mother's), on their heads. We wondered how they did it, and learned that the secret was first to place a round twist of grass on the crown of the head to act as a foundation.

Each evening, the black steward, smartly dressed in white jacket and purple fez, would pull the bunks out and make the beds. Jane was not allowed to sleep on the top one in case she fell out. I, apparently, was more expendable. Needless to say, we hardly slept; so excited were we about this great adventure, which as far as we were concerned, had already begun.

We travelled on to Mafeking, in the Northern Cape. This was originally a *kraal* (tribal village for black people, in this instance of the Baralong tribe), consisting of round, thatched huts. Mafeking was made famous in the siege by the Boers of British forces (1899–1900) in the Boer War. Then on to Johannesburg (Transvaal), the largest city in South Africa; then to the capital Pretoria (Orange Free State). Now the railway stations had Afrikaans sounding names, such as 'Nylstroom', 'Potgietersrus', and 'Louis Trichardt' (Afrikaans having developed from Dutch as a separate language following the arrival of Dutch settlers in South Africa in the 1650s). This was not surprising, for we were now in the heart of Afrikanerdom.

In the increasing heat, we were glad to avail ourselves of cold water drinks: supplied from large dispensers placed at intervals throughout the train. Finally, we were told by the African steward that we were approaching Beitbridge. Spanning the Limpopo river, and named after Alfred Beit (German-born immigrant to South Africa, benefactor of Rhodesia, and associate of Cecil Rhodes), this was the gateway from the Union of South Africa into Southern Rhodesia.

To say that the journey from Cape Town had been an uncomfortable one was an understatement. The train had a nasty habit of jolting when it reached a certain speed, as if the driver kept 'missing a gear', and therefore sleep at night had been virtually impossible. However, our hardships and privations were as nothing compared with those suffered by the early pioneers who had trekked northwards from the Cape, as will be discussed later. For them, crossing the Limpopo river had been a major feat, whereas being aboard the train, all that was required of us was to admire the view.

We had travelled halfway around the world, and the memory of what we were about to experience would stay with us for the rest of our lives. Not only that, but we were about to witness the beginning of a drama that continues to unfold, even to the present day.

Mafeking Railway Station.

4

First Impressions

Having crossed the Limpopo—by far the largest river we had ever seen—we entered our country of adoption, Southern Rhodesia. It was early May, the beginning of the 'cool' season; the 'rainy season' having ended two months previously.

It was the evening of Friday 4 May 1956 when we arrived at Bulawayo, Southern Rhodesia's second largest city (and provincial capital of Matabeleland), its name deriving, ominously, from the word 'Bulala', meaning 'to kill', and meaning 'the place of the killing'. The station platform, which was in excess of a mile in length, was one of the longest in the world. This was to accommodate goods trains: mineral extraction and ranching being the primary industries of the region.

Having changed trains, we travelled—this time courtesy of Rhodesia Railways—for the final 100-mile (or so) overnight journey to Gwelo, where we arrived at 6 a.m. on Saturday 5 May. We were exhausted after the journey and, therefore, mightily relieved to be met by Brian and Dorothy Flavell (originally from Lancashire) and their two children, Anthony and Hilary, who were of similar ages to myself and Jane respectively. The Flavells would be our neighbours, and Brian would be my father's deputy head. After the starchy officialdom of England, it seemed incongruous to see someone of Brian's status wearing shorts (father would shortly follow his example).

As we passed through Gwelo, Southern Rhodesia's third largest town, we were too tired to take anything in. However, we did sit up and take notice when the car lurched alarmingly as it passed over numerous deep storm drains, there to carry away surplus water in the rainy season.

As Gwelo receded into the distance, the tarmacadam gave way to dirt, which was thrown up in clouds as we sped along for 4 miles until, finally, our new home (a three-bedroomed bungalow, one of a number situated on a small estate at a place called Thornhill) hove into view. We had completed a journey of almost 9,000 miles—7,000 miles by sea, and 1,300 miles by land.

The bungalow had typically whitewashed walls, with a dark-red band around the base to disguise the mud, which, we were told, splashed up when the rains came.

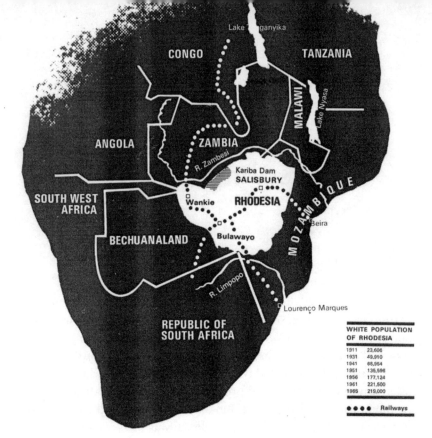

WHITE POPULATION
OF RHODESIA

1911	23,606
1931	49,910
1941	68,954
1951	135,596
1956	177,124
1961	221,500
1965	219,000

●●●● Railways

Above and below: Southern Rhodesia (map).

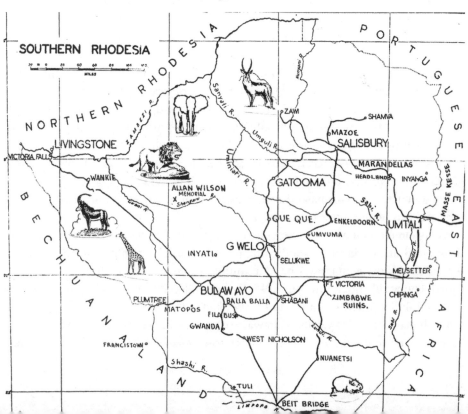

Our crates had already arrived, and although we should have rested and regained our strength, we commenced the mammoth task of unpacking them straight away. My mother held up her sheepskin coat, hung it in the back of the wardrobe, mopped her brow, and exclaimed, 'I don't think I shall be needing that!' Even though it was the cool season, it was still warm by English standards.

At the end of the garden was a building little larger than a garden shed and known as a '*kaia*', and it was from here that our houseboy/gardenboy, Timot (all black males were called 'boy', no matter what their age), emerged to introduce himself and help us unpack. His form of greeting was '*Jamba, bwana*', or '*Jamba, madam*', or in Jane's and my case, '*Jamba, piccanin baas or madam*', respectively (*Jamba* meaning 'Good day'). Like all the black people whom we subsequently met, he was polite, cheerful, and charming.

We had a pleasant surprise when an elegant-looking black man, resplendent in spotless white uniform instead of the usual khaki, arrived from the bungalow across the road bearing, on a silver tray with damask cloth, a flask of coffee and a selection of cream cakes. However, the occasion was marred somewhat by our neighbour's son, Anthony, who brought a live locust to show us—a beautiful creature, the underside of the wings of which were mauve and green—only to hurl it to the ground and stamp on it, whereupon its 'juice' squirted out onto his shoes.

It transpired that the bearer of the tray's name was Joshua: he was 'cook boy' to June Watt, the neighbour opposite. 'Just you wait until September when the leaves of the msasa trees burst forth, and the whole veld becomes a sea of red and gold!' said June, when she later came across and introduced herself ('*veld*' being the Dutch word for open, unforested grassland). Her husband, Kevin, was a solicitor in Gwelo, and we all became close friends. Dog tired, we slept well, and the following day awoke, scarcely able to believe that here we were, in the middle of Africa.

Dorothy Flavell had been kind enough to stock the kitchen with food for us, and give us some guidelines about the country's culinary customs. We soon became familiar with 'Maltabella'—composed of ground maize and malt, traditionally taken at breakfast time, and otherwise known as 'Zambesi mud'.

It was now time to explore. Our front garden was taken up with a drive and ornamental stone walls. The back garden consisted of a lawn, kept green by a water sprinkler, which contrasted incongruously with the stark aridness of the surrounding landscape. There was a small vegetable patch, enclosed by a hibiscus hedge. Beyond the garden, and an area of scrubland, lay Glengarry School (to which my father had been appointed headmaster). This was a single-storey building with long verandas (or '*stoeps*' in Afrikaans), whitewashed walls, and a red-tiled roof. A Union Jack flew from a flagpole in the forecourt to remind us all that Southern Rhodesia was a British colony.

As we settled into our daily routine, we were astonished at how quickly the sun appeared at 6 a.m. and disappeared, just as quickly, at 6 p.m. The unchanging, cloudless, pale blue skies were a novelty for those, such as ourselves, who were newly arrived from England. And how magnificent the sunsets were as the African sky turned pink, and then blood red, before the huge, orange, globe dropped slowly, and vertically down, below the horizon as if in death.

'Sundowners' (drinks at sunset) were customary, when the conversation for the women usually revolved around the servants and 'long leave' (a six-month vacation traditionally taken every three years, which gave people the opportunity to travel back to England, or elsewhere, to see their relatives and friends), and for the men, rugby (the national obsession) and roses.

Flying ants with long wings swarmed at exactly the same time each evening, and then died in droves, so that if we accidentally left a window open and the light on, they covered everything in the bungalow like a carpet. On other occasions when we made that same mistake, our home buzzed with practically every species of insect that had ever learnt to fly. We swatted them with newspapers, and by the time we had finished, the walls resembled an insect Armageddon, and required repapering in their entirety. As new arrivals in Africa, we realised that we had a great deal to learn.

Early one Sunday morning, there was a loud knocking at the back door of the bungalow. My father and mother did not seem to have heard it, so I got up, went to their bedroom door, and called out. Father answered, irritably, and duly emerged in his dressing gown, whereupon an extraordinary sight met his eyes. There, lined up across the garden, were a dozen individuals, each barefoot and attired in red and white-striped T-shirts of varying length—some almost reaching to the knee— and khaki shorts, which had clearly seen better days. At their head were two soldiers: a sergeant and a corporal, each immaculately attired in the uniform of the Rhodesian African Rifles and armed with shotguns. All were black persons. In Southern Rhodesia, there was segregation, even in the prison system, for yes, these were convicts.

'What jobs have you for my boys today, *baas*?' enquired the sergeant, standing proudly erect and beaming as my still bleary-eyed father looked at his watch and found it was only 6.30 a.m. 'Er…'—for once, he was at a loss for words. Incidentally, I noticed that as this conversation was taking place, the sergeant had given his rifle to one of the convicts ('*banditi*') to look after for him. Then my mother emerged, having heard the conversation, and quickly came to the rescue. 'What do you usually do?' she enquired politely. 'Clear the scrubland, madam?' ventured the sergeant. 'Excellent!' replied my father, seizing his opportunity. 'Yes, clear the scrubland then, if you will.' Jane and I watched, fascinated, as the *banditi* worked with their mattocks, removing every single weed in their path and hauling all the stones and rocks to one side. As they did so, they sang in unison: one of their number leading and the others joining in the refrain (our knowledge of their language, Shona, was limited, but we were told later that their songs were those of freedom and revolution).

When one of the *banditi* accidentally punctured the mains water pipe with his mattock, and a jet of water shot 30 feet or more into the air, his perspiring colleagues were agreeably surprised to find cold water spraying down on them. It was a hot day, and they frolicked about in this unexpected shower and took full advantage of it. The sergeant responded to the crisis in the typical fashion of his people, the Mashona (or Shona): he stretched out his hands, palms upwards in despair, and cried, 'Aagh!'

As his men worked, the sergeant found relaxation by sitting on a smooth stone and enjoying one of Rhodesia's most important value-for-money products—a cigarette. However, the peace was to be shattered by another untoward incident. We were having lunch when we heard what we thought, at first, to be a car backfiring, but no, in reality it was the sound of a shot being fired. A few minutes later, we saw the corporal cycling down the road with one of the *banditi* perched on his crossbar; the latter had a bloodstained bandage around his ankle. The sergeant later explained that he had been obliged to shoot when the man had tried to escape. However, he thought his wound was not serious and could easily be dealt with at Gwelo's hospital for black persons (although the terms 'blacks' and 'whites' are used in this account, in Southern Rhodesia, blacks were usually referred to as 'Africans' and whites as 'Europeans'). For those who dared to transgress against the law in Southern Rhodesia, the penalties could be summary, and harsh indeed.

From the frequency at which aircraft were seen overhead, and from the roar of their take-offs and landings, it was not long before we realised that we were living in close proximity to an aerodrome. In fact, the school, Glengarry, of which my father was headmaster, had formerly been the Royal Rhodesian Air Force's (RRAF) Officers' Mess (before the building was adjudged to be surplus to requirements).

The RRAF had started life in 1935 as the Rhodesia Regiment Air Unit. In September 1939, it became the Southern Rhodesia Air Force, which the following year was incorporated into Britain's Royal Air Force (RAF). In 1941, the Southern Rhodesia Women's Auxiliary Air Force came into being. During the Second World War, a large number of Rhodesians served in RAF Squadrons No. 44 and No. 266, including Ian Douglas Smith, a fighter pilot, who would one day lead his country. In 1954, it became the RRAF.[1]

5

School

The school that I was now to attend, Thornhill High, was situated a mile or so from our home at Thornhill. Meanwhile, my younger sister, Jane, attended Riverside Primary School, to which she travelled by bus and which was about 2 miles distant.

There were 300 or so pupils at Thornhill High: boys and girls between the ages of eleven and eighteen, and of all abilities (apart from so-called 'educationally subnormal' pupils, who attended schools such as my father's, Glengarry).

In many ways, Thornhill High was similar to a contemporary English grammar school; so much so that even the school syllabus was tailored to the Ordinary ('O') and Advanced ('A') Levels of the Cambridge Oversees Examination Board. It was for those examinations that the pupils sat. Good manners were encouraged: it being the custom for pupils to greet their teachers with a cheery 'Good morning', or 'Good afternoon, sir (or madam)', and for the boys to raise their straw boaters in acknowledgment. All pupils, whatever their faith (including Afrikaner members of the Dutch Reformed Church), were required to attend an Anglican-style school assembly with prayers and hymns. In other respects, the differences were enormous. For example, although the England of the 1950s contained, in percentage terms, very few black people, it would have been unthinkable for those who were residents of the country not to have been offered the chance to be educated in the state school system. Not so in Southern Rhodesia. Here, black and coloured people (those of mixed race) were educated separately. In consequence, Thornhill High had only white children on its register. The headmaster, Mr Philip Todd, and his staff of twenty-one were also all white.

Our classrooms, prefabricated buildings made of corrugated iron, had previously served as the RRAF airmen's billets. How many other pupils around the world had the excitement of looking out of their classroom window directly onto a runway, where, in this case, Harvard training aircraft were constantly coming and going? They were subsequently augmented by a squadron of 450-mph 'Vampire' attack jet fighters from Britain—one of which, when it first arrived, overshot the runway and

THE STAFF, THORNHILL HIGH SCHOOL

Back row, left to right: Mr. Steenekamp, Mr. Viljoen, Mr. Gibbons, Mr. Ould, Mr. McGee, Mr. Burgoyne, Mr. Taylor, Mr. Nel.
Middle row: Mr. Day, Mrs. Porter, Mrs Viljoen, Mrs. Coventry, Miss Gudath, Mrs. Bromley, Mrs. Bartlett.
Front row: Mrs. Orsmond, Miss Lamport, Mr. Holman, Mr. Todd, Mrs. Rochester, Mrs. Alexander, Miss Heath.

Thornhill High School, headmaster, and staff.

ploughed into some newly-laid tarmacadam at the far end. These aircraft displayed the traditional RAF roundel, together with three *assegais* depicted vertically across their red centres: one to represent each of the Federation's three component countries. School assembly took place in the former RRAF Operations Room in which the airmen had left behind their navigational maps that still hung on the walls. Physical training was taken in what had previously been an aircraft hangar. The concrete foundations of the airmen's former barracks served as a base for the cricket nets. When Thornhill High moved to new premises, from where the airfield, with all its concomitant activities, was no longer visible, many of us were greatly disappointed.

The boarders, who comprised roughly half of the school's membership, came largely from outlying farms. They were divided into houses which were named after two RAF training establishments back in England: 'Cranwell' and 'Halton'. The boarders considered themselves superior to us day pupils, and went around in cliques.

I had some sympathy for the Afrikaners who made up about half of our number, as they were forbidden to speak in their native tongue of Afrikaans when at school, and instead, were required to converse in the country's official language, English.

School uniform for boys was khaki shirt and shorts, black blazer with badge, silk tie, and straw boater. The girls wore pale grey pinafore dresses with short-sleeved, pale yellow blouses, and grey cardigans. However, they complained that their obligatory thick woollen ties and grey felt hats were quite unsuitable for the

Rhodesian climate. Grey socks and black, lace-up shoes were the order of the day for both boys and girls, both of whose headgear was embellished with striped ribbons of black, blue, and gold: these being the school colours. The school's motto was, '*Per Spinas ad Culminem*' ('Through Thorns to the Summit'), invented by Mr Frank Taylor the Latin teacher and mirroring the Royal Air Force's motto, '*Per Ardua ad Astra*'.

The school day commenced at 8 a.m. My journey to Thornhill High entailed a bicycle ride of half a mile or so down a road of reddish dirt. I noticed that the majority of the cars that overtook me on the way were American—it being everyone's dream to own a Chevrolet 'Bisquet' or 'Coupe Imp' (the taxis were invariably 'Studebakers'). Incidentally, there was much debate among Southern Rhodesia's motorists as to how best to negotiate the dirt roads. One school of thought was to drive slowly over the corrugations—a permanent feature caused by the rains. But the majority view was to drive hell for leather over the top of them. As I cycled along, the lifeless remains of numerous snakes littered my path—silvery creatures 2–3 feet in length, which had been flattened by passing vehicles.

The school day lasted until 1 p.m., with a half-hour break at 11 a.m. At break time, my school friends chewed strips of 'biltong' (from the Afrikaans 'bil' meaning buttock or rump, as in rump steak)—made by hanging strips of game out to dry until it attained the toughness of rubber. When, as a gesture of friendship, they offered me some, I gnawed at it politely. It was not only tough, but very salty. After 1 p.m., it was deemed too hot to be outdoors, so we were all sent home until half past three. After that, we could return to participate in sport if we so wished: for the girls, hockey and lacrosse; for the boys, rugby—which in Rhodesia (and also in South Africa) was regarded with a seriousness bordering on the fanatical. The Afrikaner boys usually played this game barefoot, even taking the conversions without the benefit of boots—for many were the sons of farmers, who were well used to going around unshod. For my part, not being particularly athletic by nature, I preferred to spend my time in other ways, such as exploring the bushveld (bush).

On Tuesdays, there was an extra afternoon session of school from 2 p.m. until 4 p.m. On that day, to while away time during the lunch break, some boys would go to the perimeter of the school grounds where they would excavate a small pit in the ground, then dig up scorpions and put them into the pit to make them fight, which they invariably did, to the death. Others, including my sister and her friends, would stroll down the road to the local garage, there to buy a fizzy concoction called 'Hubbly Bubbly', which they would drink in the shade of a trailing Bougainvillea. What luxury to have all those free afternoons. English friends back at home, eat your hearts out, I thought.

The youthful and dedicated Miss Derris Bowyer taught us French, and in addition, she gave extra lessons in that subject to anyone who might be interested. I availed myself of the opportunity, but confess to doing so primarily on account of Miss Bowyer's warm and animated personality rather than in any expectation that the language would ever be of any use to me, given my present circumstances. She married the popular, handsome, and versatile Mr W. Viljoen (affectionately nicknamed 'Doodles') who taught Afrikaans, woodwork, and physical education (PE).

Living, as we now did, in Central Africa, I naturally expected and eagerly desired to be taught something about that continent. However, my expectations remained unfulfilled. Geography teacher Mr Peter Darwin filled our heads with facts about the English Industrial Revolution, centring on the Midlands region (from where we had only recently come). Our history teacher, ex-patriot Scotsman Mr Tom Burgoyne, considered his native land to be a suitable subject for us to study; a small man, he had the habit of silently climbing onto the top of a tall cupboard from where, like some olden-time Scottish king on his throne, he bombarded us with dates of various battles—Culloden, Bannockburn, Prestonpans, and so forth—or delivered an emotional account of 'The Massacre at Glencoe'. For our part, we gained revenge on him by hiding the blackboard duster, without which (being an obsessional writer) he became thoroughly frustrated. Our English lessons were equally inappropriate to our geographical location. Here, under the stern tutelage of our form teacher Miss Sheila Pett, we were required to study Charles Dickens' *Great Expectations*; William Shakespeare's *Hamlet*; and George Bernard Shaw's *Arms and the Man*, most of which, I must confess, went above my head.

Biology was one subject which did include matters relevant to Africa: namely, the local flora and fauna. Our teacher, Miss Fletcher, could not abide pupils biting their nails, and as a deterrent to this, she kept an infant's dummy in a beaker of bitter aloes (aloe—a plant of the lily family). Anyone caught indulging in this habit was hauled out in front of the class and made to suck it—ugh! I concluded that, with the exception of my biology lessons, as far as the remainder of my education was concerned, I might just as well have stayed in England.

To signal the beginning and end of each lesson, a member of the school's Fifth Form was detailed to operate the siren—formerly used by the airman and reminiscent of the air-raid warning sirens, which, in Britain, had signified an imminent air raid by the Germans.

My sister Jane subsequently joined me at Thornhill High from Riverside. Sometimes, we were fortunate enough to be given a lift to school by the Viljoens in their luxurious Ford Fairlane saloon. They were most generous, and often stopped off at the shop on the way to treat us each to a smooth and silky 'Dairy Den' ice cream. The Viljoens owned two dachshunds, Fritzie and Freedels, which always accompanied them; their favourite trick was to sneak into the classroom, steal the rubber from its ledge at the base of the blackboard, and race away with the pupils in hot pursuit.

Jane appreciated the fact that inside the Viljoen's car, she was protected from dust thrown up from the dirt road; our local doctor having opined that this was the cause of the asthmatic attacks from which she suffered on a regular basis. Whirlwinds were another hazard, stirring up the surface of the ground and covering in dust, from head to foot, anyone unfortunate enough to be caught up in them.

My problem was migraine; intense attacks of which often came on when I was at school, and were so severe that my parents would be summoned to come to take me home. Each attack lasted, on and off, for forty-eight hours, and despite me lying in a darkened room and taking painkillers, the pain was so intense that I thought my head would explode. In retrospect, I believe that they were induced by the intensity of the African sunlight, but at the time, it did not occur to me (or to anyone else) that a pair of sunglasses might well have solved the problem.

According to the *Jumbo Guide to Rhodesia*, 'the Rhodesian African is, above all, a merry person who loves life and laughter. His laughter shakes his whole body and takes possession of all his senses'.[1] There was no one to whom this description more fittingly applied than Thornhill High's 'messenger boy' Jongwe, whose task it was to liaise between the teachers in their classrooms and the headmaster in his office. A typical scenario was when Jongwe arrived with a message—an event that we always looked forward to immensely. The sequence of events was as follows. There is a timid knock at the classroom door. 'Come in,' says our form teacher Miss Pett (all female teachers were addressed as 'Miss', whatever their marital status. In this case, Miss Pett was a single lady; she later married a Mr Coventry). The door opens, but only a crack. 'Yes, who is it?' enquires Miss Pett, knowing full well who it is likely to be—even though he chooses to remain invisible. 'Excuse me, Ma'am. The headmaster *baas*....' Finally, Miss Pett goes to the door. 'Come on now, Jongwe. Please do not be shy!' Jongwe shuffles in and stands sheepishly before the class, trying desperately to compose himself, and above all, to avoid eye contact, for he knows only too well that we will do everything in our power to make him laugh. 'The headmaster *baas*...' he stutters. 'He says to give you this message.' Suddenly, as is always the case, he can resist the temptation no longer. He looks up, and promptly dissolves into paroxysms of uncontrollable laughter. 'Heow heow heow...' This is the sound Jongwe made when he laughed, and even his hand, placed firmly over his mouth, was insufficient to stifle the bizarre sounds that emanated from it. The performance would often last for several minutes as Jongwe struggled to get his words out and we, for our part, did our best to keep him laughing.

Not only were our spirits lifted by this piece of good-natured pantomime, which served as a welcome interlude from our studies, but also Jongwe's spirits as well, for despite his discomfiture, he undoubtedly derived a certain pleasure from being the centre of attention. As for Miss Pett, I believe she enjoyed the event as much as we did, though she would never have admitted to it.

One day, we were advised that the Governor General of the Federation, Lord Dalhousie (cruelly nicknamed by us 'Lord Damned Lousy'), and his motorcade would be passing by the school. Everyone lined the roadside and cheered, but there had been heavy rain, and as his entourage drove by at speed through the puddles, we found ourselves covered in sticky, red mud, which did little to endear him to us.

When a new pupil came to join our class, he created something of a stir. His name was Courtney Ferguson, and he was a fair-haired giant of a young man, who although in his mid-twenties, was anxious to acquire some more 'O' Levels. Courtney was, in fact, a professional hunter (mainly of crocodiles), who had arrived from Bechuanaland. I wondered if he was related to Frederick Courtney Selous (who acted as chief scout and trail blazer for the Pioneer Column of early Rhodesian settlers in the year 1890) with whom he shared his name. One of Courtney's first actions was to demonstrate his great strength by taking hold of Nigel Rowlands, the head boy (with the latter's approval) by the scruff of the neck and seat of the pants, and lifting him high above his head.

Having successfully completed my 'O' Levels, there was little preamble when it came to choosing which 'A' Levels to take. The headmaster Mr Todd burst into the classroom without warning one day to enquire peremptorily, 'Now who wishes to do sciences and who wishes to do arts?' There was absolutely no discussion on the subject, let alone guidance from the teachers. What was I to do? Ah yes, the answer was simple. Wait until my closest friends had made their choice, and then follow suit. All the boys chose science. So did I. The whole affair, on which our future lives and careers probably depended, took less than a few moments.

6

Gwelo, and Further Afield:
A Tobacco Farm

Thornhill, with its airbase and small collection of bungalows—of which ours was one—was surrounded by waist-high grass (otherwise known as 'bushveld', 'veld', or simply, 'the bush'), bare in places and dotted with trees such as thorn, mimosa, mopani, wild fig, and kaffir-orange, together with anthills. Here and there lay a deserted farm, such as the one visible from our front window—a testimony to just how difficult it was to make a success of cultivating virgin soil. Now, the only plants that thrived in the vicinity of the former farm were blue gum eucalyptus trees.

Every week, my parents travelled by car—another Standard Vanguard model, which my father purchased locally—to Gwelo to do the shopping (there being no shops at Thornhill). This was a town of about 46,000 inhabitants, including 8,300 whites. Centre of the Midlands region, Gwelo was founded in 1894 on a site chosen by Scotsman Dr Leander Starr Jameson, qualified doctor, administrator of the British South Africa Company (BSAC), and friend of the country's founder, Cecil Rhodes (the BSAC was awarded its Royal Charter on 20 December 1889. Its objective was to obtain concessions from Central African tribal chiefs, in order to exploit their countries' mineral wealth and pursue other economic interests). Gwelo's name derived from the Ndebele word '*ikwelo*' meaning 'a steep descent'. This may have been a reference either to its famous '*koppie*' (hill) or to the steep-sided banks of the Gweilo River (note spelling), which ran through the town.

This was, in the main, a pleasant town with gardens, tree-lined roads, and elegant colonial buildings. On the instruction of Rhodes, the streets of all major towns had been laid out on a grid pattern, and Gwelo was no exception. In pioneering times, their dirt surfaces (now tarmacadam) had to be regularly smoothed over by an enormous metal roller made of iron, and pulled by six oxen. Not to be outdone, Jameson additionally demanded that such roads be made wide enough to accommodate a turning ox wagon and its sixteen oxen. The results were most impressive, especially when the mauve-flowered jacaranda trees, which bordered them, were in bloom.

In 1895, a Mr and Mrs Hurrell opened Gwelo's first hotel, of 'pole and dagga' construction (whereby vertical wooden poles were driven into the ground to make a circle, and then coated with a mixture of mud and cow dung). The floors were also made of compacted cow dung, which could be highly polished and possessed heat retaining properties. The roof was thatched. Shortly afterwards, in order to accommodate the prospectors who flooded into the area in search of gold, six more hotels were built.

Mrs Hurrell owned one of the few pianofortes in the country, which was in great demand for use at open air concerts. She was also involved in a project to build Gwelo's memorial swimming baths (public, but for white people only), located in Gwelo Gardens (public park) together with a bowling green, both believed to be the first of their kind in Central Africa.[1]

Buildings of note included the Old Stock Exchange (1898), the Magistrates Court (1905), and the Town Hall (believed to be of a similar date). Minerals were abundant in the region, hence the presence of ferro-chrome, iron, and cement works. Furniture and clothing were also produced here; and footwear, by the firm Bata. The most notable landmark was a memorial clock, erected by Mrs Jeannie M. Boggie, an early settler, in memory of her late husband, about whom more will be said shortly.

As we began to travel farther afield, the influence of the Dutch was to be seen everywhere: 'Afrikander' oxen, with typically humped backs and large horns; bilingual road signs, such as 'Keep Left' and underneath this, '*Hoo Links*' (Afrikaans, which we at first thought meant 'Golf Course'); and elegant buildings with Dutch-style gables.

For Rhodesians, favourite holiday resorts were Beira, a sea port in Mozambique at the mouth of the Pungwe river or Durban in South Africa. However, it was in Natal that a tragedy occurred, which was reported in the *Rhodesia Herald*. The report was about a Mr Paul Brokenshaw, a Southern Rhodesian farmer:

[Brokenshaw] saved a 14-year-old Bulawayo schoolgirl Julia Painting, from a shark in the waters off the Natal coast, by attacking the creature with his bare hands. The announcement that his action had won him the George Medal was made in the *London Gazette*.... When the shark was sighted at Margate, Natal, all bathers quickly left the water with the exception of Mr Brokenshaw and the girl. The shark made its first attack and seized the girl, bit her, and mauled her side before wheeling around for a second attack. As Mr Brokenshaw saw the shark return he caught hold of its tail but it threw him off. He returned to the attack, wrestling with the shark and raining blows on it with his fists. He tried to grab the girl away from its grip, but her swim-suit came off in his hands. The shark severed the girl's left arm and then made off. Mr Brokenshaw pulled her into shallow water and carried her to the beach. His brave action was instrumental in causing the shark to leave its victim, who would have lost her life without his intervention.[2]

This event both shocked and saddened the nation, and led to a special fund being established for the victim, to which we all contributed.

One half-term, my family was invited to spend a week on a tobacco farm, situated near to Southern Rhodesia's capital city of Salisbury. The farm belonged to Colonel Dick McGill and his wife (known as 'Fluffy'), whose son, Richard, was a pupil at father's school, Glengarry.

Seemingly endless rows of the tobacco crop (which resembled spinach, except that the leaves were considerably larger) were visible in all directions, as far as the horizon; the only interruption being where lines of trees had been planted, at intervals, to serve as windbreaks. Tobacco was traditionally harvested around Christmastime. We were shown into enormous sheds where the leaves, having been hung up to dry, turned from green to yellow, and where a large number of black women were engaged in grading it, according to its quality. They then tied it into bundles to be crated ready for auction. In the words of the 11 March 1958 edition of the *Rhodesia Herald*:

> The 1958 tobacco auction sales will be opened at 9 am today by the Governor-General Lord Dalhousie, on Tobacco Producers' Floor [in Salisbury]. The preliminary estimates set this year's crop at 168,000,000 lb. It is likely to yield more than £20,000,000 to the Federation.[3]

I had it in mind that, one day, I might train to become a doctor. How ironic, therefore, that here on the tobacco farm, I should find myself in the midst of what was in effect, a gigantic poison factory.

Colonel Dick told us that the cultivation of tobacco in southern Africa had begun in 1719, when Cornelis Hendriks was sent out to the Cape from Amsterdam to supervise matters. The first European to grow tobacco in Rhodesia was Dunbar Moodie in the 1890s. It was not until 1902 that the crop was first cultivated, commercially, by a Dr Sketchley who had previously grown it in Fiji. Salisbury, now, was the largest single marketing centre for tobacco in the world (although the US was a larger producer overall).[4] Cigarettes were currently priced at one halfpenny each, and advertised incessantly on the radio, accompanied by a musical jingle, which went in English: 'Westminster eighty-five, smoke Westminster eighty-five, just as sure as you're alive, you'll like Westminster eighty-five,' and was then repeated in Afrikaans.

On the farm, said the Colonel, it was considered good etiquette for black persons and white persons always to acknowledge each other: the customary greeting being '*Jamba, baas*' or '*Jamba, bwana*' on the one side, and 'Good morning', or whatever was appropriate, on the other. Each would then enquire as to the health and well-being of the other's family members, including wife, children, grandchildren, parents, grandparents, and so forth, and only after these formalities had been observed was the business of the day discussed.

Horse riding was *de rigueur*. 'Do be sure to keep your horses well behind Richard's,' said Fluffy, his mother, to Jane and me. His 'has a jealous nature and does not like being headed.' At first, all went well. Jane's horse, however, although smaller than the other two, was wilful, and despite her best efforts, it suddenly rushed to the front, with the dire consequences that Fluffy had predicted. Richard's horse immediately broke into a gallop and did not stop for half a mile. He was fortunate not to have been thrown off!

In the evenings, following the traditional 'sundowner', everyone—children included—would retire to the lounge. One evening, as the Colonel and my father smoked their cigars, the former, to our surprise, enquired, 'Why are the natives black all over their bodies, with the exception of their palms and soles?' He proceeded to answer the question himself, by relating the following story:

Years ago, there was a river, and God decreed that all those who reached this river before midday, and immersed themselves in it, should have a reward—their skins would turn white, and this is precisely what happened to those who got there first. However, as you know, the Blacks are naturally idle fellows who dislike getting

MUNICIPALITY **OF GWELO**

His Worship the Mayor (Councillor J. R. Cannon) and
Councillors of Gwelo
request the pleasure of the company of

Mr. and Mrs. C.A. Norman

at a Sundowner to be held at the Hellenic Hall at 6.15 p.m.
on Thursday, the 20th February, 1958,
at which His Excellency the Governor-General,
Simon, Earl of Dalhousie, G.B.E., M.C., and Lady Dalhousie
will be present.

Invitation to Sundowner.

up in the mornings, so by the time they got to the river it had almost dried up. All they could manage to do was to immerse the palms of their hands and the soles of their feet.

Fluffy was of the same opinion: 'You see, it's quite simple really!' she said triumphantly. 'But that is a legend, surely?' I said, feeling compelled to speak, even though children were normally supposed to be seen and not heard, particularly when they were guests in someone else's house. There followed a long and sometimes heated discussion, which lasted until the small hours of the morning—Jane and I, for once, being allowed to stay up late. I argued that the Colonel's story simply did not make sense—not least from a scientific point of view. Years later, when the full impact of Charles Darwin's theory of evolution by natural selection had dawned upon me, I realised that this would have been the ideal weapon with which to refute such absurd claims.

The Colonel, for his part, was not prepared to give an inch. Whether he was testing me, or whether he genuinely believed the story, I did not know. The following morning, I met my father on the stairs. He had remained largely silent during the debate of the night before, and I was apprehensive as to what he might say. At the very least, I could expect a severe dressing down. Not at all. To my surprise, he beamed at me and whispered, 'I was really pleased with the way you conducted yourself last night, son,' which from him was praise indeed.

Before we left the McGills, an event occurred that might well have turned into a tragedy. On a nail on the wall of Richard's bedroom had hung, since the end of the Second World War (in which the Colonel himself had fought), Colonel Dick's Army service revolver. Anxious to show me how the gun worked, Richard took it down, removed it from its holster, and, believing the chamber to be empty, held the barrel in his left hand and pulled the trigger with his right. There was a deafening bang, and when the smoke cleared, there was blood everywhere. It might have been much worse, but miraculously the bullet had passed between his middle and index fingers, causing no more than a flesh wound. Richard's mother, Fluffy, also had a narrow escape: she had come to summon us for tea, and had been standing in the doorway at the very moment the shot had been fired—the bullet having passed into the door frame above her head.

7

Leisure

It was a treat to be taken by car in the evening to Gwelo's drive-in cinema ('bioscope'), to watch such films as *April Love*, starring Pat Boone; Elvis Presley in *Jailhouse Rock*; or, for the more adventurous, *Angels One Five*, which was about the Second World War's Battle of Britain. Otherwise, my school friends and I would congregate to play our latest gramophone records—usually American. Two friends, in particular, Robin McGowan and Lawrence Boddington, were adept at jive and rock and roll, and what better music to perform to than Bill Haley and His Comets' 'Rock Around the Clock'? During the hours of daylight, however, it was always the great outdoors that beckoned.

Gwelo was supplied with its water and hydroelectric power by the nearby Whitewaters Dam, which we often visited at weekends with our friends, Robin's parents, Vincent and Joan McGowan. Vincent was superintendent of the nearby dam at Gwenoro. Adjacent to Whitewaters Dam was a swimming pool. To have swum in the dam itself would have been folly, due to the risk of contracting the disease bilharzia, caused by a parasitic worm of the family *Schistosoma* (and named after German researcher Theodor Bilharz who first discovered it in Cairo in 1851).[1] Our neighbour's son, Anthony, who contracted bilharzia through imprudent bathing, was ill in hospital for many weeks.

For this reason, all water, including that provided for swimming pools, came either from purified central water supplies or via boreholes from underground streams, and was therefore perfectly safe either to swim in or to drink.

Robin and I were given permission to take the McGowan's motorboat for a trip up the reservoir created by the dam, having been told distinctly not to venture out of sight. Robin, who was in charge, immediately opened the throttle of the 'Johnson' outboard engine and headed straight for the river that fed the dam. As we chugged nonchalantly along, I noticed the unmistakable shape of a small crocodile swimming alongside. I pointed it out to Robin. 'Don't worry, man,' he said, 'That one is only a baby.' 'It's not him I'm worried about,' I replied. 'It's his larger relatives!' I knew that one flick of an adult croc's tail is all that would have been required to turn the boat over and hurl us into the water, when the results would have been entirely predictable (the crocodile first drowns its prey I was told, and then hides the body in the bank until it is sufficiently mature to be consumed). Robin, blanching at the thought, hastily swivelled the engine round, and in a trice we were heading back to safety. As we docked, we noticed a snake wriggling about in the water. It was a water snake—long, bright green, and venomous. Up until then, I had not realised that snakes could swim. We relaxed and watched as lizards, 3 feet or more in length, with brilliant turquoise or yellow undersides, darted across the sun-baked rocks from one granite boulder to another.

Visits to Whitewaters Dam were always an excuse for a barbecue (*braai vleis*— 'roasted meat' in Afrikaans), which in turn provided an opportunity for singing. To my mind, there are no more moving songs than those traditionally sung by the Afrikaners. My favourite, about a young lady called Sarie Marais, was in fact popular at the time of the Boer War, and the haunting words of its chorus never failed to stir my emotions. It was usually sung in Afrikaans, of course, to the accompaniment of a guitar; the English translation being as follows:

> *My Sarie Marais is so far from my heart*
> *But I hope to see her again*
> *She lived in the area of Mooi-river*
> *Before the war began*

[Chorus]

> *O bring me back to the Old Transvaal*
> *Where my Sarie lives;*
> *There by the maize*
> *By the green thorn tree,*
> *There my Sarie lives.*

During our excursions, we had to be careful to treat the African sun with the respect it deserved. As an indication of its intensity, one had only to see how even the thickest towels, having been washed and hung out on the line, dried within minutes in the shimmering heat. Despite our precautions, however, my mother's ankles continued to swell badly on account of the heat, and she also suffered from earache: said by the doctor to be caused by a blockage of the Eustachian tubes, brought on by the altitude.

It was a tradition for the pupils of Thornhill High to stage, in Gwelo's Hellenic Hall, an annual production of a Gilbert and Sullivan operetta. Our producer was the music teacher, a delightful, but somewhat excitable Greek lady called Mrs Nikki Antoniadis. In *HMS Pinafore*, I fulfilled a lowly role as a member of the chorus, in which capacity I was obliged to stand on the deck of the 'ship' for half an hour or so clutching a live chicken. The part of Ralph Rackstraw was taken by our Latin teacher, Frank Taylor, who possessed a fine tenor voice, and Head Girl Gaye

Robertson was Josephine. We were not exactly awash with competent singers, as this comment from former pupil Sally Callaghan (*née* Struckel) indicates:

> There were a few of us boarders (who sang like frogs in a tin pot) who were not even picked for the chorus. They debated whether we should be included and [told us] just to keep our mouths shut, or be left out altogether. The latter was decided, because of the expense of [hiring] the costumes.

Although we considered the whole affair something of an incongruity, I must confess that the lyrics and melodies, as sung by 'Little Buttercup' and 'Sir Joseph Porter, K.G.B., First Lord of the Admiralty', have remained with me all my life. The following year, my sister fulfilled a similar role as I had done in *The Pirates of Penzance*. Tickets for such performances were always a sell-out, and everyone had tremendous fun.

When Thornhill High challenged its neighbour, the Royal Rhodesian Air Force, to a swimming competition, we schoolboys would have been beaten out of sight had it not been for my classmate Robin McGowan. Here was a fine swimmer, who held both Rhodesian and South African backstroke records. Not surprisingly, therefore, Robin found himself entered for every single race, including the relay and diving—his 'swallow dive' was a sight to behold, combining power with gracefulness. The pupils were duly victorious, and the exhausted Robin was hero of the hour.

On another occasion, my visit to the swimming pool was a less-than pleasant experience. Three friends and I were in the water when we heard a high-pitched, and ever-increasing, whining noise. Somebody called out, 'Dive man, and hold your breath as long as you can!' I took the advice given, but when I surfaced, desperate for air, I was stung in the face—twice. Before submerging again, I quickly glanced around. Everyone had left the pool side and was running for dear life to seek shelter in the changing rooms, for the sky was black with a swarm of angry African bees! One small boy had unfortunately tripped and fallen down on the path by the pool side. Before he could be rescued, he received more than twenty stings. An ambulance was summoned, which rushed him to Gwelo Hospital. He was lucky to survive.

A popular excursion was to nearby Selukwe, the picturesque town having been established in 1904 on the eponymous goldfield (here were also to be found substantial deposits of high-grade chrome ore).

In this region of relatively high rainfall were to be found hills, forests, and farms, and in spring, a glorious array of msasa trees cloaked the countryside in a canopy of red, plum, and mellow gold—just as our neighbour, June Watt, had predicted. A favourite picnic spot was Ferny Creek, where the sound of water cascading down its various waterfalls made a refreshing change.

It was at a ranch near Selukwe that Rhodesian farmer and politician Ian Douglas Smith was born and brought up. Educated at Chaplin School, Gwelo, and Rhodes University, Grahamstown, he served as an air force pilot during the Second World War in the 'Rhodesia Squadron'. In 1953, he became Member of the Federal

Parliament for Midlands District where we lived, and of which Gwelo was the capital town.[2]

Perhaps my greatest joy of all was to visit, in company with my friend, Barry Poulsom (whose father was headmaster of nearby Guinea Fowl School), a farm belonging to an elderly lady, Miss Cousins. She would generously provide us with a pair of ponies, together with a .22 rifle, and off we would go into the bush, firing at anything that moved (I feel somewhat relieved now, in retrospect, that we never actually managed to hit anything).

Thornhill airbase was a hive of social activity, and one December day, the commandant and his wife, Wing Commander A. D. G. and Mrs Wilson, invited my parents to a pre-Christmas dance there. Evening dress was mandatory, and the dance would commence at 20.30 hours (half-past eight to us). My mother said she was especially looking forward to it, and told us later how much she had enjoyed it, though the same could not be said of my father.

A young RRAF officer had been detailed to look after my parents, and he duly followed them about, dutifully replenishing their glasses whenever the need arose. Favourite drinks of the day were whisky, brandy, and 'Castle' or 'Lion' lager. While my father indulged in animated conversation, his glass was topped up frequently with spirits, something which he was not used to: the result being that first he

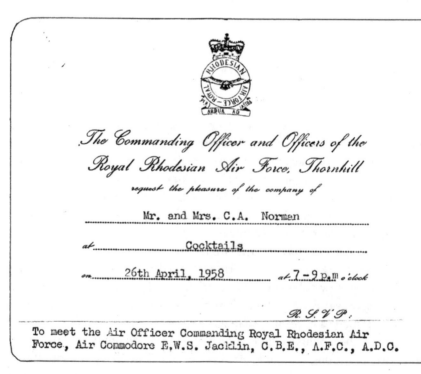

The Commanding Officer and Officers of the
Royal Rhodesian Air Force, Thornhill
request the pleasure of the company of

Mr. and Mrs. C.A. Norman

at Cocktails

on 26th April, 1958 *at* 7 – 9 p.m *o'clock*

R.S.V.P.

To meet the Air Officer Commanding Royal Rhodesian Air
Force, Air Commodore E.W.S. Jacklin, C.B.E., A.F.C., A.D.C.

RRAF invitation.

became happy, and then so miserable that halfway through the festivities he sought my mother out and said he wanted to go home. She, however, was taking a rare opportunity to enjoy herself on the dance floor, where, as an attractive woman, she was in great demand with the young airmen. Meanwhile, her advice to my father was for him to sit down for a while and rest, and drink some water. Finally, they left, even though they had been invited to stay right through until morning, when breakfast would be laid on.

Jane and I would normally have gone to bed, but it so happened that this was the night when one of the Russian Sputnik satellites (of which there were two in orbit at that time) was due to pass overhead.[3] We therefore stayed up and sat on the *stoep*, passing the time watching 'shooting stars'. This was a phenomenon which occurred every few moments, each one describing an arc as it fell, lighting up the clear heavens like a Roman candle in one brief glimmer of glory before it burned itself out. 'Father! Mother!' we exclaimed when my parents returned, 'You are just in time. Any minute now and we shall see the Sputnik!' 'I don't care a damn,' said my father, who was clearly the worse for wear. 'They can keep their ruddy Sputnik!' We stood in amazement as he staggered past us and inside through the back door. Never before had we heard him swear, let alone seen him drunk. A few moments later, a tiny dot of light appeared and travelled slowly across the clear, African sky.

The Officer Commanding Southern Area

requests the pleasure of the company of

MR AND MRS NORMAN

to a parade

to celebrate the occasion of

the Official Birthday of

HER MAJESTY THE QUEEN

at the Drill Hall ground

GWELO

at 9.30 am on Thursday the 12th June 1958.

RSVP: Adjutant,
Central Africa Command Training School,
P.O. Box 734,
GWELO.

Dress: Lounge Suit
or Uniform.

Invitation to birthday parade.

On the second Saturday of June each year, the townspeople of Gwelo were thoroughly preoccupied with celebrations to mark the official birthday of Her Majesty Queen Elizabeth II. For the invited guests, my family included, there was to be a march past, followed by speeches from Governor-General Lord Dalhousie, Prime Minister Sir Roy Welensky, and Mayor of Gwelo Mr J. R. Cannon. To record the event for posterity, my father handed me his new Japanese Samoca 35-mm camera, which he had acquired on the advice of a friend, having been greatly impressed by it possessing the novel facility of a 'coupled rangefinder' for manual focussing. This was a great step-up from my modest Kodak box camera (for which colour film was prohibitively expensive), but not as grand as a cine-camera that only the most affluent could afford.

Confident that my father would settle for nothing less than a comprehensive record of every group that marched by, I stationed myself at a suitable vantage point and began to film. 'Click, click, click', went the camera as I filmed the Guides; the Scouts; the Brownies; the Round Table; the Loyal Women's Guild; the Royal Rhodesia Regiment (descended from the Pioneer Corps of 1890, Rhodesia' first citizen soldiers); the Rhodesian African Rifles; the British South Africa Police; and the school bands of Guinea Fowl, Thornhill, Que Que, and so forth. Finally, just as the film ran out with the taking of the salute and the playing of the National Anthem, my father came rushing up to me. He was about to be introduced to the Governor-General—what an honour. He therefore asked me to take a photograph. 'But Father, there is no film left,' I stuttered plaintively. His face turned to thunder. We had no spare.

Usually, when our colour slides came back from the developer, everyone looked forward to the ensuing film show. On this occasion, however, nothing was said, and as far as I know the subject was never mentioned again.

8

Flora and Fauna, including Snakes!

With every new day came new discoveries. The butterflies: 'Diadem', 'African Monarch', 'Swallowtail', 'Mother of Pearl', and 'Charaxes', to name but a few, were a revelation; as were the magnificent 'Hawk' and 'Emperor' moths, which were liable to fly into the bungalow at night if we were ever careless enough to leave the light on and the window open.

Praying mantises were commonly seen among the foliage, well-camouflaged by their green or brown colour. Described as the gardener's friend, they feed on grasshoppers, flies, and caterpillars. The female grows to a length of 3 inches; the male being smaller, but with large wings that enable it to fly freely (unlike the female whose wings are small, and therefore useless for flight). The praying mantis is aptly named, for its posture really does give the appearance of supplication. However, the long, spiked forelegs are designed, not for praying, but for ensnaring its prey. To the Biblical commandments, 'Thou shalt not kill' and 'Thou shalt not commit adultery', the female is entirely oblivious: for having performed her nuptials with several mates in succession, she then proceeds to make a meal of them, each and every one.

We had not seen white ants before, but sure enough, here they were. In fact, there was once a saying that in Southern Rhodesia, everything was owned by the white ants and Thomas Meikle—he was one of the brothers who opened a general store in Fort Victoria in 1892 and another in Gwelo in 1894. This was the start of a business empire comprising a retail chain and also a chain of hotels, including the famous Meikles Hotel in the capital Salisbury (which opened in 1915, and where Southern Rhodesia's first Parliament met in 1924). The Midlands Hotel in Gwelo was part of the Meikles chain.

When a cloud of locusts arrived (I had been warned they might), I stared in disbelief as, before our eyes, they began to demolish the cabbages and lettuces that our houseboy/gardenboy, Timot, and I had tended so lovingly all season. He and I both laboured frantically, fighting a losing battle to remove them from the plants, which they were so voraciously attacking. For Timot, however, there was a hidden agenda: he suddenly disappeared into his '*kaia*' and emerged with a cooking pot. 'Nice to eat!' he proclaimed joyfully, and began filling it with the unfortunate locusts. It is an ill wind, I thought.

Locusts were not the only intruders. One evening, my father and mother were relaxing in the lounge when my mother exclaimed, 'Chris, listen!' My father, who seldom paid attention to anything she said, looked up irritably from his newspaper, the *Rhodesia Herald*. 'What is it?' he snapped. 'I can't hear anything.' 'Will you listen?' said my mother, 'I'm sure there is something moving about outside.' 'Don't be silly dear. Of course there isn't. Now if you don't mind....' From the rear of the house came the sound of heavy breathing. My father jumped up from his chair and strode purposefully to the back door and flung it open (a rash thing to do in the circumstances, for in Africa, one was never quite sure what was likely to be prowling about). No sooner had he stepped outside the door than he shot back in again, slammed it firmly behind himself, locked and bolted it, and collapsed against the washing machine looking deathly pale. 'Are you alright dear?' enquired my mother anxiously. Suddenly, we became aware of an enormous Afrikander cow with big brown eyes and a huge pink tongue staring in at us through the window. When my father had recovered his composure, he told us it had had the impertinence to lick him, the headmaster of Glengarry School, on the nose. The cow, which had obviously strayed from a nearby farm, had not had a wasted journey, for the following day, Jane and I ruefully inspected the stumps that were all that remained of our broccoli.

Trees flowered in August–September, just before the coming of the rains. In the corner of our garden was a Frangipani (a species originating from the West Indies and named after a fifteenth-century Italian count of that name), exquisitely scented and with porcelain-like pale yellow flowers.

In the grounds of my father's school were acacia trees shaped like umbrellas, whose scented flowers of brilliant yellow were exactly matched in colour by the tiny weaver birds that used their branches from which to suspend their nests. The Cassia (or 'candle') tree was also a favourite with its yellow, cone-shaped clusters of flowers.

As already mentioned, the streets of Gwelo were lined with jacarandas, and its roundabouts planted with cosmos (known in England as 'cosmea'). In Salisbury, however, each street had been deliberately planted with a particular variety of flowering tree, confirming what the guide book said:

> If you come to Salisbury in spring or summer you will be aware of why it is called the 'city of flowering trees'. Endless avenues of jacarandas spread a cool blue haze over the warmth of October. Then, and suddenly, in a blaze of scarlet glory come the flamboyants; vivid, orange-trumpeted spathodias; purple, mauve-and-white bauhinias; sweetly-scented peach and white frangipani; the massive red, yellow, pink and white flowers of the poinsettia and cascades of bougainvillea.[1]

With the coming of the rains, there were yet more wondrous sights to behold when the landscape (including the normally monotonous veld) exploded into colour. In our front garden, there was a stone wall with raised border, which now brimmed with colourful zinnias, cannas, and tall blue agapanthus (we were careful to avoid this area, as it was rumoured that a snake lived here). Passion flowers (granadillas) produced elongated, purple-coloured fruits that were delicious to the taste. The hibiscus hedge was a wonder, with its beautiful five-petalled crimson flowers in the shape of trumpets. It was here that Jane would deposit her pet chameleon for the night, before collecting it and placing it in its customary position on her jumper the following day.

On account of its slow and deliberate movements, the chameleon was nicknamed '*Hamba Gahle*'—'proceed carefully'—by members of the Zulu people. These lizard-like creatures with their sharp toes for grasping and long tails can change colour automatically (to brown, green, yellow, or black) to match that of their surroundings, and thereby camouflage themselves against the threat of predators. Their tongues can be thrust out to a length of 6 inches (equivalent to its body length, excluding the tail), and at such lightning speed that their insect victims are impaled on their sticky tips before they know it. The chameleon's eyes each work independently, enabling it to focus simultaneously on two different objects. What would the decision-making process be, I wondered, if two tasty morsels appeared simultaneously from opposite directions—or two enemies, come to that?

The 'prickly pear', which is not a pear at all, has lobular leaves and wicked spines, with flowers of red or white at the edge of the leaf (a spineless variety was grown for cattle feed). Red hot pokers ('torch lilies') bloomed in suburban gardens in July—provided they were kept well-watered. However, their natural habitat was the veld, and they also thrived in *vleis* (hollows where water collected in the rainy season). Our neighbours prided themselves on their red and purple bougainvilleas, which they trained up the walls of their bungalows, along with dazzling blue-flowered 'morning glory'. On the journey to Gwelo, one could not help but marvel when the cosmos came into flower, and the traffic islands were bathed in colourful drifts of gently swaying pink, mauve, and white. It seemed paradoxical for such wonderfully coloured flora to coexist with the scorched orange and brown of the bushveld.

The speed with which plants grew was truly amazing. I broke off a twig from a mulberry bush and planted it in the garden, and within a year, it had grown to a height above that of the guttering of the bungalow. Ednam and Joan Dudley who farmed at Mazoe, 25 miles north of Salisbury and whom we met, showed us photographs of orange trees that they had grown from seed (pips). By the second year, they were 10 feet tall, and by the third, they were bearing fruit.

Surely, the most fascinating bird to watch is the weaver. The male is bright yellow with a black face (whereas the female is dull yellow), and it is he who builds the nest. Before work can commence, however, it is first necessary for him to loop, over the end of a drooping branch, a length of grass from which the nest is suspended—like a bauble on a Christmas tree. Finally, in order that he might have a clear field of vision, should a predator approach, he strips the branch of all its leaves. Soon, we were to experience the plight of one particular weaver bird at first hand.

The 'Garden of Eden' would not have been complete without its snake, and here were snakes a-plenty. In fact, snakes were everywhere, and we accustomed ourselves to being watchful and to walk 'head down', or 'head-up' if we passed under a tree. At the entrance to Glengarry School stood an acacia tree (the sweet thorn acacia, with the scent from its yellow flowers hanging in the air, was common in most parts of southern Africa), and one day I saw some of the school children staring up into its branches. What were they looking at? At first, I could see nothing unusual, but suddenly there was a darting movement. A long, yellowish-green snake was stretching out for one of the many weaver birds' nests. However, the plucky little male weaver will attack any snake on sight, and judging by the cacophony of sound emanating from above, this is precisely what was happening.

'Boomslang!' muttered Hendrik, one of the older pupils of Glengarry School ('*boom*' being Afrikaans for tree, and '*slang*' meaning snake, hence tree snake). The boomslang's staple diet is lizards, mice, and small birds, but it is particularly partial to birds' eggs, and this was the laying season. Well adapted for robbing nests, it curls its tail around the branch of a tree and is thus able to extend the forepart of its body for a considerable distance. 'Is it poisonous?' I enquired. 'Ya, man, extremely poisonous,' he muttered gravely. 'I go fetch Mr Nel'—he was the local policeman. In Southern Rhodesia, a country where it was often necessary to make lightning decisions, it was customary to omit from the sentence any word considered to be superfluous.

My father arrived, hot foot, on the scene, and quickly ushered the children away from under the tree. Soon Mr Nel—otherwise known as 'Tiny' on account of the fact that, like so many Afrikaners, he was a large man who stood about 6 feet 4 inches in his socks—appeared with his rifle. His first bullet struck the snake a glancing blow. This was followed by four direct hits: with each one the wounded creature writhed in agony, dropping from branch to branch in its death throes. Finally, it landed on the earth at our feet. The snake had lain out in the heat of the sun for an hour or so when someone suggested that we measure it. We did so and found it to be 4 foot 10 inches long—marginally less than the record length for a boomslang. If only we had thought to do this earlier, before it had shrunk in the African sun.

The puff adder, which grows to about 3 feet in length, is so-called because of the way it puffs out its neck prior to making its lightning strike. Then, with a hissing sound, it bites, delivering its deadly venom through hollow, elongated, backward-pointing fangs. The snake eats only at intervals of several weeks; its jaws expanding with ease to accommodate a large rat or even a chicken. Whereas most snakes prefer to glide away when they sense the approach of a human being, the sluggish puff-adder has a habit of lying still among rocks, in grass, or even out in the open on a pathway—hence the danger. We read in the *Rhodesia Herald* about a man who was bitten by one. His whole leg turned black and he was seriously ill for many days, despite being hospitalised and receiving antiserum. Fortunately, we never encountered a puff-adder in the wild, although one was kept by our teacher Miss (Mrs) Fletcher, in the biology lab at school. Neither did we ever see the legendary, fast-moving black mamba.

Miss Fletcher lived on a farm, where her husband was constantly obliged to shoot the pythons that came to raid the chicken-run. In fact, the skin of one of these unfortunate creatures was visible to all, because she had pinned it, trophy-like, to the wall of the biology lab. According to the record books, the longest specimen of a python ever to be recorded was 25 feet, and this one was not far short of that. Its skin was dark brown with shiny scales and a fascinating, reticulated pattern.

Miss Fletcher brought a young, live python into school, and kept it in an old tea chest. It refused to eat dead white mice, so it was fed a diet of live ones. Then one day, when the python had become accustomed to her handling it, she took it outside, and as we stood in a circle, she placed it in the centre on the grass and said blithely, 'Whoever it approaches may pick it up.' To say I was thankful when it avoided me was an understatement! Each of us then took it in turns, under Miss Fletcher's instruction, to drape it around our necks, being careful to keep a firm hold of both ends (pythons are not poisonous, they kill by constriction, and this one was 5 or so foot long, so we were not taking any chances).

Pigs were kept at Glengarry School and looked after by the children who fattened them up on leftovers from the kitchen before they were sold to the local butcher. One afternoon, when there was no one else about and the school children were having their customary early afternoon rest, I decided to visit the pigs in their enclosure, which was situated near the playing fields at the rear of the building. Suddenly, and for no apparent reason, I stopped, and it was as well that I did, for lying motionless at my feet was a snake, jet black, as long as I was tall, and as thick as my arm, if not my leg. Paralysed with fear, I now knew the meaning of the phrase 'rooted to the spot'. Finally, I managed to put one foot behind the other and withdraw to a safe distance. Then, I raced to the school as fast as my wobbly legs could carry me. My father telephoned for Mr Nel, but by the time we returned, the snake had gone. 'They'll never believe me,' I thought, looking at the multitude of staff and pupils who by now had congregated at the scene.

A few yards from where I had seen the snake was a compost heap, and Mr Nel said he felt sure that this was where we would find it. He, therefore, persuaded my father to stand on top of the heap and poke around with a garden fork, while he pointed his gun, ready to shoot if it should appear. My mother looked at me accusingly, and I read her thoughts. By breaking the rules and venturing outside in the heat of the day, I might well now be held responsible for the death of my father, who would either be bitten by the snake, or accidentally shot by Mr Nel.

Thornhill High School pupils studying the snakes during a biology class. Left to right are: Ann Torry, Miss E. Fletcher (behind), Gaye Robertson and Roy Davies. Ann Torry and Gaye Robertson are holding a python.

SCHOOL KEEPS CAGES OF SNAKES

Midlands Reporter

Gwelo, Monday.

EVEN in Africa a box-full of home-grown snakes in a school science laboratory must be a rarity. At Gwelo's Thornhill High School there is a cage of boomslang, puff adders, cobras, night adders and a skaapsteker.

In an adjoining cage there is a long and energetic — but seemingly friendly—python.

All the snakes are very much alive and all were caught in the grounds over two terms. This is not as ominous as it sounds for the school is a new one and the grounds until last year were mainly bush.

Today, snakes are seldom seen on the new lawns and freshly made flower beds.

Most of the snakes were captured by the children, some by the African garden staff and a few by the science mistress, Miss E. Fletcher.

Bright lights are being shone into the cages to prevent the snakes, now very small, from hibernating. The light increases their feeding rate and their rate of growth.

Above left: Thornhill High School: pupils with python. *From left to right*: Ann Torry, Miss E. Fletcher (at rear), Gaye Robertson, and Roy Davies. (*Photo: Gwelo Times*)

Above right: Andrew on 'stoep' with snake.

Fortunately, neither event occurred. We never did find the creature, but Mr Nel said he believed it may have been a mole snake: a constrictor that lives on rats, moles and lizards and which (unlike other snakes that lay eggs) gives birth to live young, up to forty at a time. We often found snakes' eggs in the bush. They were not oval and hard like birds' eggs, but malleable and wrinkled.

9

Wankie Game Reserve

At Wankie (so-called after a local black chief of that name) in the north-east of Southern Rhodesia, were huge reserves of coal: production at its mines (which had been in operation since 1903) being in excess of 4 million tons per year. However, the pride and joy of the area was its magnificent game reserve, covering an area of some 5,000 square miles (five times the size of England's county of Dorset). There were no physical boundaries, and the animals within it were free to wander at will. According to the guide book:

> … credit to the idea that thousands of acres should be set aside for the creation of game reserves belongs to the late Major W. J. Boggie [husband of Jeannie, whom we would shortly have the pleasure of meeting], a man of many parts, who grew [had grown] alarmed at the effect of an expanding civilization on Rhodesia's wildlife. He [had] expressed his anxiety to the Legislative Assembly and gave the example of a hunter who had just shot 170 buffalo and five lions in the Wankie area.[1]

The major had gone on to describe Wankie:

> [It was] the most ideal place [for a game reserve] in the whole of the country; game was extremely prolific and there were no native inhabitants except primitive Bushmen; the pans ['pan'—a shallow depression in the ground in which water collects—colloquially known as a 'watering hole'] contained abundant water, especially towards the close of the rainy season.[2]

The major's comments about Bushmen surprised us for, as far as we knew, there were none at Wankie nor anywhere else in the country in the Southern Rhodesia of the 1950s. As a result, the Wankie Game Reserve was officially created in 1928.

The Robins Rest Camp, where we stayed, was adjacent to the house where zoologist and hunter, the late H. G. Robins FRGS, FZS, had once lived; its tall observation tower

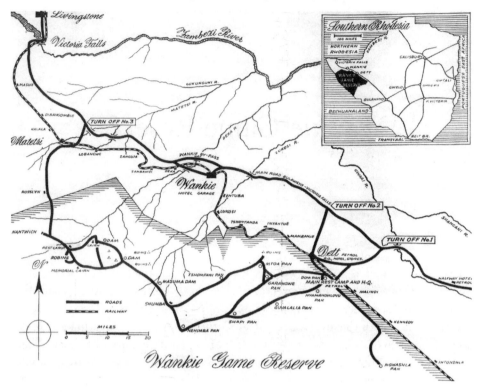

Above: Wankie Game Reserve.

Left: Wankie Game Reserve—warning notice.

commanded an extensive view of the surrounding countryside. It was he who had created the adjacent 25,000-acre Robin's Game Sanctuary, which was 'maintained for 25 years for the protection and preservation of game'. When Robins died in 1939, he bequeathed his sanctuary to the people of Southern Rhodesia, and as his reserve shared a common border with Wankie, the two reserves were amalgamated.[3] Said the guide book: 'The best months are August and onwards, when concentrations of game at the artificial water holes increase as the dry season continues'. It was therefore a fortunate coincidence that this was the month that we chose for our visit.

> The area is liberally criss-crossed with watercourses and there are a number of large natural pans. The most frequented of these are the Nyamandhlovu and Guvalala, which are particularly rich in the minerals for which most animals have a strong craving. The best time for game viewing is early morning and late afternoon, out of the heat of the day.[4]

As visitors, we were accommodated in a *rondavel* (round house with thatched roof, of similar design to a native village hut except that the walls were made of brick, rather than dried mud). The day began at 6 a.m., or thereabouts (this varied according to the time of year). The routine was for us to venture out for a couple of hours and then return for a hearty breakfast, cooked by the black attendant. Driving along the reserve's sandy tracks at that early hour was to be an unforgettable experience. At first, it was so quiet and empty-looking that we began to wonder if there were any animals to be seen here at all. There was no 'dawn chorus' of birds as we had been accustomed to back in England.

The dirt roads, which ran through scrub of varying density and height, were winding, unlike the main roads, so there was always an element of suspense. What would we encounter around the next bend? As we drove along in the car, my parents in the front, and Jane and I in the back, we vied with each other as to who would be the one to spot something of interest first.

Our first sighting was of a herd of zebra about 200 yards away. On seeing the car, their reaction was to stop browsing and simply stare at it. We noticed that perched on the backs of the zebras were cattle egrets (otherwise called 'tick birds'), which were pecking away to remove the ticks that had attached themselves to the zebra's skins. A giraffe came into view: a tall, majestic creature, which strolled unconcernedly among the acacia trees. Surely, this was Africa in all its glory.

Some extracts from my diary, written in fountain pen in a 'Croxley' exercise book—or *Skryfboek* in Afrikaans—will give an idea of the variety and abundance of the reserve's wildlife:

Tuesday 20 August 1957: Rest Camp

We encountered a small herd of zebra, but they were very frightened and galloped away. I saw a baby duiker [small antelope], in the bush. It was about 10ft away from us. We saw six kudu buck [alternative name for antelope]. Then, turning a corner, two large ostriches, and a giraffe. At Tshebema, we saw lots of waterbuck walking by the pans. There were vultures, and near the trees, lots of little monkeys.

Although there was a speed limit of 20 mph in the reserve, the warning was superfluous, for as the sandy surface became softer, it was an effort for Father to keep the car from skidding, or getting stuck. 'Watch out! Something's run out in front!' shouted Mother. 'What is it?' said Father irritably, for as yet, the offending creature had not entered his field of vision. 'I don't know!' she said. 'Well what did it look like?' 'Look like…?' Mother struggled to find the correct adjective, and failed. 'Well … like a piggy thing. Can't you see? Look, its running alongside the car!' It transpired that the creature, which emerged safely, was an adult warthog, which, seemingly undisturbed by the event, trotted happily away with its tail in the air. After that, warthogs were invariably called 'piggy things'.

Wednesday 21 August: Robins Camp

We arrived at Shapi Pan just before sunset, to view the animals as they arrived for their evening drink. Here, we pulled up alongside twenty or so cars, which were lined up on a specially created viewing rampart, with a game warden's Land Rover parked at either end of the row. The pan was immediately in front of us, surrounded by an area of open space leading to dense scrub.

There was only one animal there—a large giraffe, which walked up and down the side of the pool, waiting for the others to come. Eventually, he stopped, put his front two legs astride, bent his long neck, and had a drink. After about ¼ of an hour, a big giraffe came along, with its baby, and had a drink. The first one ambled off. Several more followed, all on the alert, pausing at intervals to sniff the air.

We saw some people looking to the right through binoculars, and in about five minutes, some 200–300 buffalo came to drink. They were rather shy at first, because three ladies were standing out in the open and talking loudly and excitedly. In about five minutes, the game warden drew up and told them to get in their cars. A duiker buck came down to the water, drank, and the giraffe ambled away. Then, on the opposite bank, two waterbuck came along and also had a drink. Suddenly a man, in a car next to us, pointed to the left.

A large bull elephant appeared, trumpeting loudly—we were told that the elephant population of the reserve exceeded 2,000. He was evidently the forward scout of the herd, for in the distance, to our left, there appeared a cloud of dust which heralded the approach of a family of a dozen or so of his colleagues. This was followed by another family, and yet another, totalling seven herds in all.

Despite the great size and destructive power of the elephant, it was noticeable how gentle and protective these creatures were towards each other, and especially

A lone giraffe.

towards the calves, which were invariably shepherded into the centre of the group for their protection, with each one holding on with its trunk to the tail of the one in front as they trundled along. Approaching ponderously, a step at a time, they did not hesitate to enter the water, and as soon as they did, the fun began, as they rolled about playfully and squirted one other.

The elephant's playtime was now to be cut short as the buffalo, their leader boasting a magnificent pair of curved horns, sidled cautiously but determinedly towards them, a few paces at a time. Whenever he stopped, so did all the others. Finally, he and his herd reached the water's edge, by which time the elephants had moved across to confront them. An excited murmur emanated from the occupants of adjacent cars, for a drama was about to be played out under our very noses.

There developed a battle of wills as the elephants and buffalo jostled each other for position. For a while it was stalemate. In the cars, the atmosphere was hushed with anticipation. My guess was that the elephants would prevail, on account of their greater individual bulk, but I was wrong, for it was they who retreated in the face of the seemingly endless tide of buffaloes. This indicated to us what we had previously been told: that the buffalo is a beast of fearsome reputation, which, if provoked, can cause immense damage with its sharp, scything horns.

It was getting late, so we hastened away, only to have to wait as another herd of elephants crossed our path.

On a narrow track, where overtaking was impossible, the car in front of us suddenly stopped, and lo and behold, there, not 50 yards away, was a huge, solitary bull elephant. He looked uneasy. So did we. We tried to reverse, but our wheels failed to grip the sand. The regulations strictly forbade us to get out of the car. We were trapped. The elephant approached even closer, waving its head menacingly from side to side. Then it began tearing up saplings, and trumpeting. We were terrified. Finally, my father could stand it no longer. He leapt out of the car, rushed to the one in front, and shouted through the open window, 'For goodness sake move on, will you!' The woman driver glared at him reproachfully. 'Shush!' she said. 'Please do not shout, or you will wake the baby!' Her infant, oblivious to the drama, was sleeping soundly in its cot on the back seat.

On our return to the rest camp, we saw several more giraffes and noticed many uprooted trees—clearly the result of elephant activity. By the time we arrived back at camp, it was dark.

At night, we slept under the customary mosquito nets. Once, we were woken by a coughing sound, and next morning, our black steward told us that a leopard had been seen lurking behind rocks at the rear of the camp. The leopard, which has a distinctive cough, is a nocturnal animal that hides away during the day in thick cover, or inside a rocky cave. In order to catch its prey, it frequently lies in wait up on the branch of a tree. Although we were never fortunate enough to see a leopard, we often saw carcasses of antelopes, which the spotted cat, with its prodigious strength, had dragged up and wedged high in the branches. Here, his or her next meal was safe from other predators; to be consumed at will at a later date.

Wednesday 21 August Robins Camp.

We went from Robins on the Circular Tour, and felt very depressed because all we had seen were a few small buck. We arrived back at camp and a man cheered us up by saying that he had seen a pride of lions, eight miles away on the Windmills Road. [Some people we spoke to, regular visitors to the reserve, had never had the good fortune to see a lion, the creatures being well camouflaged, and exactly the same colour as the parched grass.] We immediately set out, and on the way saw duiker buck, together with tsessebe, warthog, zebra, sable antelope, and many guinea fowl.

We saw some cars ahead and drew up alongside them. We looked to the right and saw a large tree with a bush under it. Under the bush was a large, dead antelope. We saw the lion and several cubs in the bush just to the left. The lioness was also there.

Family groups of lions, we were told, tend to remain within the same area. The lion or lioness usually attacks prey at night, preferring to rest and conserve energy during the heat of the day, while the dead carcass matures.

We waited and one of the cute little cubs grew impatient. He got up, walked over to the carcass, and sniffed it. The lion opened a sleepy eye and growled. When another cub did the same, the lion growled again, slightly louder this time. When a third cub, even bolder, went up and scratched at the dead antelope's skin, this was a step too far. The lion leapt up, gave a mighty roar, and cuffed it with his mighty paw. The little cub cowered, and retreated. Then the lioness took the cubs off into the bush and the lion stayed on guard.

There was evidently a strict pecking order: the male lion feasted first; the females and the cubs being obliged to wait their turn.

Suddenly, to our astonishment, the male occupant of the car in front got out in order to take a photograph. This, despite there being large notices everywhere saying 'DO NOT LEAVE YOUR CAR. IF YOU BREAK DOWN, A GAME WARDEN WILL FIND YOU BEFORE LONG'.

The lion assumed a crouching posture. Seemingly oblivious to the danger, the man continued filming. Then, in a single bound and with a speed that had to be seen to be believed, the creature covered in a trice, half the distance between himself and the man, who fled for his life back into his vehicle. The lesson from this was that whereas the animals in the game reserve were used to vehicles, and ignored them, human beings out in the open were quite another matter.

I recalled reading in the *Gwelo Times* the reprint of an article that had first appeared in that newspaper in the year 1916. It was a vivid account of an early settler's encounter with a lion. The person involved was Jim Harris, who owned gold, coal, and asbestos mines, both at Shabani, and at Que Que, where he was proprietor of a store at the Moss Gold Mine.

Lion, lionesses, cubs, and 'kill'.

Jim was at home asleep one night with his wife, Lily, and their infant son, George, when they were awakened by a commotion. Jim rushed outside with his shotgun, only to come face to face with a lion. Realising that such a weapon was useless against an animal of this size, he rushed back inside for his rifle, only to find that he had run out of cartridges. He could only observe from the window as the lion, together with its two companions, proceeded to kill and eat their donkey and mules. The lions then left the scene. When, the following afternoon, a native brought news that the lions had been located, Jim, together with the elderly Mr Hogg, manager of the Moss Mine, set off in pursuit, for they knew that having paid one visit and tasted blood, the predators would surely return. Lily now took up the story.

> They [Jim and Mr Hogg] walked quite suddenly on to three of the brutes. Mr Hogg fired, and killed a huge male lion with a beautiful shot. Jim wounded one, and Mr Hogg fired again and wounded another. At this, Jim begged him to come back as he himself had only one cartridge left, but the old man, who was fearfully excited, said 'Oh, just one more!', and fired and missed. The lion sprang on Mr Hogg and grabbed him by the shoulders. Jim bravely stood his ground and fired his last remaining cartridge through the lion's stomach, at which the beast dropped Mr Hogg and sprang on poor darling Jim.
>
> Jim says he (the lion) charged him like the fastest racehorse ever seen, his mouth wide open, ears laid back and roaring. Jim actually fought him; then he put up his arm to save his face. The brute grabbed him by the arm. Jim suddenly thought of lying flat as though dead; he says he also prayed. The lion took a bite out of each of the dear boy's hips, and just very slightly scratched his back, and then rolled over. Jim says that for quite a minute or two they lay together like this, then the lion got up and slunk away to die.

Lily did not mention her own subsequent bravery in venturing out into the night on her bicycle in order to find her husband—the neighbouring white men having declined to accompany her as they were too afraid. When she did find him, at a distance of 2 miles from the house, she bathed his wounds with Condy's fluid (a weak solution of potassium permanganate) and 'poured whisky into him'. Mr Hogg, however, was unable to drink, being too far gone. Eventually, help arrived and both men were admitted to hospital in Que Que. Mr Hogg, sadly, did not survive the night.

It was fortunate for Jim that the lions had feasted off the mules and the donkey the previous night, and their teeth had therefore been cleaned by the flesh of the animals. Otherwise, it was almost inevitable that anyone who was bitten by a lion and survived went on to develop a fatal septicaemia, caught from the putrid flesh attaching to its fangs.

When Jim Harris died in September 1949, 4,000 members of the Ndebele people, attired in full ceremonial dress, did him the honour of attending his funeral. '*Bayete*!

Bayete!' they cried, in a salute normally reserved for a chief, for to them, a man who fights with a lion is a hero.[5]

Many years later I was to see, in London's Hunterian Museum, a replica cast of the humerus (upper arm) bone of missionary Dr David Livingstone who, during his early years in Africa, was attacked by a lion. This left him with a badly damaged humerus, which became infected and never healed. When Livingstone died, it took a year for his remains to be brought back to England. By this time, severe decomposition had set in, and positive identification was only possible from the damaged humerus. Several casts of the bone were made from the skeleton, another of which is in the possession of the Royal College of Physicians and Surgeons of Glasgow, the city in which Livingstone had previously trained to become a doctor.[6]

The abundance of game was astonishing—especially of antelopes. Eland were the largest and springbok perhaps, the most nimble, but my favourite was the sable with its black body, white belly, and spiral-shaped horns; herds of 200–300 of which being by no means unusual.

Baobab (or 'cream of tartar') tree with lookout post.

10

Timot

I guessed that our houseboy/gardenboy, Timot, was in his early thirties and suspected because of his Biblical name ('Timot' being short for Timothy) that he had been educated at one of the many mission schools. In fact, black people were almost invariably known by such names, given to them by the missionaries—'Solomon', 'Kephas' (derived from Caiphas), 'Elias' (Elijah), 'Moses', 'Shadreck', and so forth, rather than by their African tribal names.

Timot's attitude to life in general was epitomised by the modern-day phrase 'laid-back'. The concept of time was expressed by him in a vague, yet delightful way. 'Tomorrow' could mean, literally, what it said or next week, or next year—and 'yesterday', the reverse. About his friends, he was equally vague. 'I am seeing my brother' could serve either for the past, the present, or the future. I realised from the many male visitors he had to his *kaia* that it was impossible for him to possess so many brothers, so I assumed that these people were members of his extended family or tribe, or simply friends of his. For those who offended him, however, Timot had a choice word, '*skelm*' (which he pronounced, with relish '*skelem*'), meaning a rogue. '*Bobajohn*'—meaning monkey—was also a term of abuse, used by both black persons and white.

In the mornings, my mother would extract the slumbering Timot from his *kaia*— in which he would otherwise have slept for most of the day—by calling out 'Timot, *ena funa wena*!' meaning 'Timot, I want you!' This is 'Kitchen Kaffir', or to give it its correct name, Fanagalo—a simplified language incorporating native, Afrikaans, and English components.[1] Of Fanagalo, we quickly acquired a smattering, and I confess that there were occasions when I mimicked my mother's words in order to trick Timot into getting out of bed even earlier. We soon found words of Fanagalo replacing those of our own language: for example, 'the toilet' became known as '*the piccanin kaia*' or 'little house'.

Timot was renowned for his absent-mindedness, and when he failed to fulfil a particular task to which he had been alloted, my mother would chivvy him along. '*Tshetsha! Tshetsha!*' ('Quickly! Quickly!') or '*Manje! Manje!*' ('Now! Now!').

When the plants in the garden were dry, which they usually were, it was 'Timot, *hamba tata lo manzi yabulisa*' ('Timot fetch water, please'), whereupon Timot would fill the watering can and await further instructions. '*Tela manzi!*' said my mother, becoming exasperated. 'Pour water!' When my father pointed out to Timot that had he taken the trouble to water them, the tomato plants might not have withered and died, he merely rubbed the back of his neck with his hand ruefully, as if this was something that had not occurred to him. I sowed some radishes and peas, taking particular trouble to show Timot exactly where I had sown them. The following day, he dug over the entire area, having forgotten what I told him.

Initially, we had been surprised, not to say somewhat shocked, to see how Timot and others like him lived: in tiny two-roomed *kaias*, with just enough space for a bed, a hole in the ground for a toilet, and running water supplied by an external garden standpipe. As for his diet, compared to ours, it was meagre and monotonous. Like all black servants, he was given 'mealie meal' (ground maize) three times a week, and fresh meat, usually stewing steak, twice a week. The fact was that while we were by no means rich by European standards, Timot had virtually nothing to his name except for an iron bed with mattress and blankets; a so-called 'missionary pot' (for cooking) made of cast iron and having three legs; and a catapult, a penknife, and some wooden animals, carved by him out of sapele wood. However, all too quickly we became assimilated into white Rhodesian society and came to accept this as the norm.

Despite suffering these privations, Timot remained of cheerful disposition, and was sometimes even known to be a little boastful. Flexing his biceps, he would say, in his clipped English, 'Timot, he have muscles like Jake Tuli' (the black South African boxer of some repute) and then, getting me to do the same, point to my inferior ones and chuckle with disdain. I once asked him to provide evidence of his self-proclaimed great strength by knocking down a brick garden wall with his fists. 'How much you pay, *baas*?' I felt in my pocket. I only had a '*tickie*'. He laughed. 'You must pay Timot one hundred pounds, then Timot knock wall down!' He then invited me to feel the sole of his foot, which was so hard it could resist all but the sharpest of thorns. Like his comrades, he seldom wore anything on his feet.

Timot had teased me about my inferior muscles. Now it was my turn to tease him. I knew he was in fear and dread of chameleons, so when we were in the back garden, I took his arm and guided him towards the hibiscus hedge where one had attached itself to a branch. His eyes widened, his pupils dilated, and he bolted into his *kaia*. The reason for this, which I did not know at the time, otherwise I would have acted differently, was as follows: according to native legend, the chameleon was a gift sent to man by God to bring immortality to mankind. In contrast, however, the lizard, which was subsequently sent by God with the opposite message—one of death—was faster and reached man first. Therefore, due to the chameleon's slowness, man lost his chance of immortality. Hence, Timot's fear of any association with that creature.

Although Timot was supposed to help my mother with the domestic chores, she had reservations, both about his efficiency and his standards of cleanliness, so she ended up doing virtually everything herself (the start had not been a propitious one, for on the very first day of our meeting with him, when he was helping us unpack the wooden crates containing our belongings, he had accidentally broken a valuable moustache-cup that had once belonged to my mother's great-grandfather, and possibly to his father before him). One day, finding the vacuum cleaner missing from its usual place in the hall cupboard, she asked Timot if he had seen it. '*Aziko lapa, madam*,' ('there is nothing here') said he, stretching out his arms, hands palm upwards. 'Go and look again,' said my mother. '*Nikis*,' ('nothing') answered Timot. She finally discovered the appliance standing outside the back door next to the dustbin. 'Madam, sweeper no good! Sweeper no work!' Timot did not realise nor could he have done so without being shown that it contained a bag, which, when full, required emptying.

I knew my father was anxious about what the neighbours might say about me becoming too friendly with Timot, not only because he was a black person, but also because he was our employee. I also noticed that when I mentioned the subject at school, there were disapproving mutterings, and someone even called me a 'Kaffir lover'. Nevertheless, I found Timot to be an entertaining companion, whose knowledge was invaluable when we commenced our regular excursions into the bush. Also, I loved his sense of humour. I therefore decided to continue to cultivate his friendship, even if I had to do so surreptitiously.

I learned from Timot that it was necessary, when walking in the bush, to keep to the recognised tracks, otherwise 'ticks'—blood-sucking insects—were liable to detach themselves from the grass, and latch onto one's legs (for ticks, the legs of animals were equally fair game). Despite our precautions, we would often return from a walk to find several ticks sticking to us, their bodies blue and bloated almost to the size of grapes with our blood inside them. If one simply pulled them off, they invariably left their jaws behind in the flesh, which could set up an infection, and the only successful way to remove them was to hold a lighted cigarette up against them. As a preventative, I tried wearing long socks (not ideal in the searing heat), but Timot, wisely, refused my offer to lend him a pair, for now 'black jacks' (long seeds with hairy hooks) became a problem, and were almost impossible to remove from one's clothing.

On one of our excursions, we came across a cluster of anthills, each between 4 feet and 6 feet in height. Timot told me that the fine soil out of which they were made was highly sought after, and used to make the base of tennis courts. I thought he was joking, until one day, such a court was built for Glengarry School, and this was the material used.

We often encountered bare patches of scrub, littered with the bones of cattle that had died and been picked over by vultures. When these great, sinister-looking birds circled high in the sky, this was an indication that some poor creature had met its death, one way or another, and that they would shortly descend and scavenge on its raw flesh.

One day, we found a skull, complete with horns, and presumably that of a cow (though I preferred to think of it as 'big game'). Anxious to have a trophy to hang on my bedroom wall, I persuaded Timot to help me drag it all the way back to the bungalow. We hid it behind his *kaia*, and when my parents were out, hauled it into my bedroom, where I suspended it above my bed by a string from the picture rail. That night, the household, myself included, was awakened by a deafening crash. The string had snapped. My father, furious, came rushing into my bedroom. 'What in the devil's name have you been up to now?' he said.

I asked Timot if he was married. Yes, he said, and told me that his wife and *piccanins* lived some miles away in a *kraal* on the Native Reserve. I told him I should like to meet the members of his family, and he promised that one day he would introduce them to us. His habit was to visit them once a month for the weekend, when on a Saturday night, the air would reverberate with the sound of drums that were clearly audible from the bungalow. We imagined Timot and his friends having a party and dancing, singing, and enjoying their home-made 'Kaffir beer'—an alcoholic liquor made from fermented Kaffir corn (sorghum or millet). I sometimes saw Timot returning to his *kaia* on the following Sunday evening, unsteady on his feet and with glazed and bloodshot eyes—the result of his merrymaking.

True to his word, Timot brought his wife and *piccanins* to see us. Their features were soft and rounded, with beautiful brown, conker-coloured eyes and thick, black, curly hair so typical of the Shona people. While my mother scurried about looking for unwanted clothes to give to 'Mrs Timot', and made up little food parcels for the children, Jane and I shared our sweets with them.

Timot's son, Joshua, aged five, was playing on the scrubland between our garden and Glengarry School when he was bitten by a snake. He calmly came into the garden and showed me the two puncture marks on the tip of his finger. My father was summoned by telephone and he arrived at the scene post haste, while Timot was urgently dispatched to search for the offending serpent—doctors preferring to see both it and the patient together for the purposes of identification. Timot failed to find the snake, so my father, accompanied by myself, rushed Joshua to the hospital for black persons. We raced along the dirt road, dust blowing up in our wake, and feeling sick with anxiety. 'Was the snake venomous—most were not, it was true—and if so, will we get there in time to save him?' Having handed the unfortunate Joshua over to the doctor, my father telephoned my mother, but Timot had still not found the snake. The doctor administered antiserum and told us that, to be on the safe side, he would keep Joshua in hospital overnight for observation. To our great relief, the little boy survived, none the worse for his ordeal.

We returned from what my father called 'a run' in the car to find Timot standing in the driveway holding in his outstretched hands a velvet cushion upon which rested, not the Crown Jewels of England, but my sister's pet angora rabbit, 'Flossie'! As the car drew to a halt, Timot thrust the cushion in through the back window, right under Jane's nose and announced peremptorily, '*Piccanin madam*, your rabbit, him dead!' Was it my imagination, or was there a look of expectation in his eye, and

Above: An African village—'*kraal*'.

Below: Timot, his wife, and *piccanins*.

a ghost of an anticipatory smile on his face? Jane screamed. Whether the rabbit had died of natural causes, or whether Timot had assisted it in shrugging off its mortal coil, will never be known. Whatever the truth, I felt certain from the look on Timot's face that he saw the lifeless corpse, not from Jane's perspective, but as a potential meal. However, whatever hopes he may have entertained were swiftly dashed by my mother, who, in an effort to console the distraught Jane, announced that we would hold a special burial service in the rabbit's honour. Jane could make a little cross out of twigs, after which we would all join together in prayer. Jane duly fetched the trowel, and a suitable site behind the frangipani tree was decided upon. The service was attended by Timot himself, who quietly pointed out to me with ill-disguised mirth that, in her haste to bury 'Flossie', Jane had inadvertently left the tips of the creature's hind legs sticking up out of the ground.

Timot was always delighted to receive a *basela* (Fanagalo for 'a gift'), or at Christmastime a *kisimus* ('Christmas gift' or 'Christmas box'). He was to feature in a hilarious episode that occurred on the occasion of the birthday of our neighbour, Dorothy Flavell, who had been given not one, but two pairs of carpet slippers as presents. Choosing the pair she liked better, she donated the other pair, which were pink with fluffy bobbles on the toes, to her houseboy Shadreck; the idea being that he would pass them on to his wife when she next came to visit. Dorothy was, therefore, astonished, when on looking over our garden fence, an incongruous sight met her eyes. Timot was not only wearing the aforesaid pink slippers, he was prancing up and down the lawn in obvious delight at them. She tore round to our bungalow and banged on the door in a state of high dudgeon to upbraid my astonished mother in her broad Lancashire accent (which in the middle of Africa, sounded somewhat incongruous). Having learned that he had 'done a deal' for the slippers with Shadreck, Dorothy cried, 'That Timot is a plausible rogue!' and from that day forth the epithet stuck.

There was a further furore when Dorothy caught Timot wearing one of her husband's discarded shirts, and practically exploded with rage. She clearly regarded Timot as a bad influence, and it was no coincidence that shortly afterwards, she replaced the hibiscus hedge between her garden and ours by one of napier fodder, which she allowed to grow to a height of some 8 feet. She also padlocked her back gate to dissuade the 'plausible rogue' from communicating with her precious Shadreck.

Timot did have some consolation, however, as I discovered when I saw him pulling a small furry creature, possibly a vole, out of a hole by its tail. '*Gundwun!*' he said gleefully. 'Nice meat!' and sure enough, a few minutes later, I saw a wisp of smoke issuing from the chimney of his *kaia*. Snakes were also considered a delicacy.

There was an occasion when my friendship with Timot almost landed us both in serious trouble. One afternoon, when school had finished, as usual, at 1 p.m. and my parents and Jane had gone into Gwelo to do some shopping, I decided to call on Timot at his *kaia*. 'Are you there?' I asked, poking my head around the door. There was no reply. I called more loudly. 'Timot, are you there?' 'Eh, *piccanin baas*?' He emerged slowly, wiping his bleary eyes. I had obviously woken him from slumber.

For Timot, that morning had been particularly stressful. My father had enquired of him, somewhat pompously, 'In your language, how do you say, "You smell very much!"', to which Timot replied sheepishly in Kitchen Kaffir, '*Maninge nuka.*' (Why father required the translation escaped me, for Timot understood English perfectly well. In fact, Timot's native language was Karanga—a dialect of Shona.) 'Well, Timot, I say to you, "*Maninge nuka*". Why have you not washed today?' At this, I felt sorry for Timot. After all, the only washing facilities available to him were his small ablution room and the outside standpipe (which happened to be situated in the centre of a bed of arum lilies, which I forever associate in my mind with him).

As if he did not have trouble enough, Timot now began to moan and point to his mouth: '*Tshisa lapa skop!*' For the severe toothache that he was now experiencing, the choice was either to attend the hospital for black people at Gwelo or to seek the advice of the local witch doctor (who employed mainly herbal medicines and had great influence on the black community as far as health was concerned). Timot, however, decided to do neither. Instead, he went to my mother, who made him a concoction of medicine ('*muti*'), which included aspirin. He also asked for a bandage, which he proceeded to wrap right around his head, from crown to lower jaw, giving a somewhat bizarre appearance. I attempted to cheer him up. 'Look! I've made a new catapult,' I said. 'Come, we go to the *koppie*!' 'Come, we go' was a nonsensical phrase that I had picked up from my schoolfellows, one of whom had provided the elastic for the catapult, obtained from the discarded inner tube of a motorcar tyre.

At first we could find nothing to aim at. Then, suddenly, there was a rustling sound, and a pheasant emerged and obligingly ran along the path in front of us. I fired, but only succeeded in flicking the rubber against my hand. 'Ouch!' 'Give it to me, *piccanin baas*,' said Timot, and despite his somewhat groggy condition, he killed the pheasant, instantly, with a single shot to the head. 'Whew, pretty good!' I said admiringly. 'Shall we cook it?' Timot's eyes lit up. For him, this would make a pleasant change from his normal diet of beef and mealie meal.

I ran to the bungalow and found some matches. Then we made our way to the back of the *koppie*, and while he gathered some sticks for kindling, I began clearing a patch of grass. We suspended the pheasant on a branch, and lit a fire underneath it. Unfortunately, we had not reckoned on the wind, which in a flash, carried the flames into the tinder-dry grass. We tried to beat the fire out, but it was hopeless. 'Come on, let's get out of here!' I said, and we returned another way, so as to approach the bungalow from the opposite direction. No one must suspect.

We reached home and Timot crept furtively away to his *kaia*. I cautiously opened the back door. My mother was in the kitchen, looking pale in the face and staring wide eyed out of the window. Said she:

Andrew, I have had such a shock! I was sitting in the lounge reading my magazine, when the sky went quite dark. I was astonished. I could not imagine what had happened. Then, one of the boys came and told us the bush was on fire!

A Schoolboy Expedition

The Sabi River rises in Northern Rhodesia, flows down through the then-Southern Rhodesian province of Mashonaland and the foothills of its Chimanimani Mountains, crosses the border into Mozambique (also known as Portuguese East Africa), and finally into the waters of the Indian Ocean, which it joins near the port of Bartolomeu Dias.

The Lower Sabi (River) Expedition of September 1958 was sponsored by the Rhodesian Schools Exploration Society (Patron-in-Chief, Rhodesian-born barrister and judge the Honourable Sir Robert Tredgold, KCMG), and I was among the twenty-five schoolboys fortunate enough to be chosen to participate in it.

The aims of the expedition (which, needless to say, was for white schoolboys only), were set out in the expedition's official report:

1. To encourage the spirit of adventure, self-reliance, self-discipline, friendship and leadership in schoolboys, by the organization of expeditions or explorations for the senior boys of Rhodesian schools.
2. To ensure that each expedition or exploration has definite aims, involves investigation in a scientific manner, and returns with accurately recorded data and a collection of appropriate specimens.[1]

The area to be explored was situated 7 miles above the confluence of the Sabi and Lundi Rivers, and only 5 miles from the border with Mozambique.

Leader of the exhibition, which was organised by the Midlands Branch Committee, was Mr T. A. Magness, headmaster of Jane's former school, Riverside. The party included eight other schoolteachers (leaders) and officials, twenty pupils, and a black staff consisting of one cook, two cook's assistants, two skinners (of zoological specimens), and one native department messenger (interpreter).

My school, Thornhill High, was represented by the geography teacher Mr Peter Darwin (the expedition's quartermaster and also its Honorary Secretary), and pupils Lawrence Boddington, Robin McGowan, and myself. Other schools represented

In the circumstances, I thought it best to remain silent. In a strong wind, the flames from a bush fire can travel at great speed, and if the wind veers, may change direction and be a mortal danger to any creature—man or beast—in the vicinity. There were, therefore, severe penalties for starting such a fire. Fortunately, there was still no sign of my father. 'Surely, you must have noticed?' said Jane to me accusingly. 'Look at his face, Mother! I bet he's got something to do with it.'

I peered out of the window and through the smoke. Buck, fleeing for their lives, bounded across from the opposite side of the road, which, we hoped, would act as a firebreak for, by now, the flames were fast approaching. Then came wild cats, rabbits, and hares—all, desperately, trying to get clear. Finally, and much to my mother's disgust, came rats, hundreds of them; by which time the black employees, both of the school and of the local farm, were out in force, ready with their knobkerries, and anxious to kill them for the pot. The sky teemed with birds, which were seizing their chance to prey upon the grasshoppers and other insects driven out by the flames, as they, in turn, were preyed upon by hawks circling at an even greater height above. 'Where is Father?' I enquired, nervously, of my mother. 'First, he telephoned the police to warn all the neighbouring farms, and now he's gone up to the *koppie*.' 'Come on,' said Jane. 'Let's go and see for ourselves.'

In the distance, we could see a line of black men desperately trying to beat out the flames: a hopeless task as the whole landscape, as far as the eye could see, was rapidly being burnt to a cinder. The fire would only stop when it reached either a man-made windbreak or a river. I knew the school and our bungalows were safe because they were protected by the *koppie* and the adjacent playing fields (which typically, this being Central Africa, did not possess a single blade of grass). When we reached the 'scene of the crime', the evidence was still all too apparent. 'Look,' said Glengarry schoolteacher Mr Staniforth, holding the pheasant aloft. 'A native has been trying his hand at cooking!' That evening, my father announced that he intended to assemble all the pupils and staff together the following day, and give them a lecture on the dangers of 'veld' fires.

A month later, when the dust had settled—both literally and metaphorically—I thought it best to own up. By then, the ground was already beginning to recover and would soon be ablaze with Rhodesian flame lilies. How paradoxical that such beauty could emanate from so barren a landscape.

There was one happy outcome, however. Mr Nel, the local policeman, was strolling through the charred remains of the bush when he came across a baby duiker antelope, which had miraculously survived the flames and showed no sign of distress. He took it home, built a wooden hut and pen for it, and invited Jane to visit every day and feed it on milk from a baby's bottle. Its ears were as smooth as velvet and Jane nicknamed it 'Bambi'. When the antelope grew strong enough, Mr Nel released it back into the wild, where we could only hope that it managed to be reunited with its parents once more.

THE CHRONICLE, WEDNESDAY, SEPTEMBER 3, 1958

MAYOR SAW
THEM OFF

Rhodesian Schools Exploration Society

REPORT

ANDREW NORMAN

HADEDA IBIS

LOWER SABI EXPEDITION

September, 1958

The Mayor of Gwelo, Mr. J. R. Cannon, chatting with the leader of the Schools Exploration Society expedition to the lower Sabi, Mr. Bill Magness, before the expedition set off from Gwelo.

Above left: Sabi River Expedition. Setting off. Mr J. R. Cannon (Mayor of Gwelo), Mr Bill Magness (leader), Andrew (aboard truck). (*Photo: Gwelo Times*)

Above right: Sabi River Expedition: Report.

were Riverside, Guinea Fowl, Que Que, Chaplin, and Fort Victoria. Major H. B. Blowers organised the transport and operated the radio.

Gwelo's Round Table helped finance the expedition with fundraising activities, including a charity football match. It also canvassed local shopkeepers and businesses (including Rhodesian Castings Ltd, and Rhodesian Sugar Refineries) who generously donated virtually all our equipment, food, and stores. Private individuals were equally generous, and loaned us the following vehicles: a 5-ton open-back Bedford truck (to transport 'the lads'); a 25-cwt Bedford van (described as 'the old riot wagon' and driven by Mr Darwin); a Land Rover (to be driven by Gavin Judge, our tutor in forest botany); a De Soto vanette (to be driven by our medical officer Dr C. R. Deuchar); and a 7-ton lorry (to transport the main bulk of our food and equipment). The pharmaceutical company Winthrop, based in Salisbury, provided anti-malarial drugs; Pfizer and Eli Lilly donated antibiotics.

After a preliminary reconnaissance by two of the expedition's leaders, the native commissioner (government official responsible for administration at a local level) for Chipinga, Mr E. Streak, generously placed his camps at our disposal, and one of these at Mahenya was chosen as being ideally suitable for a base. It was reported:

… the camp, a clearing on the east bank of the Sabi River, roughly 75 yards by 50, was tree-shaded and sheltered by low *koppies*. At its foot flowed the river, a shallow but fast-moving channel of water 100 yards wide in the sandy river bed nearly a quarter of a mile in width. Crocodile and hippo spoor (tracks and traces) abounded, an indication that the dangers of the Bush should not be taken too lightly, even though all the game in the immediate vicinity had been shot out by John Jenke's tsetse fly-control hunters. [Jenke, formerly of the British South Africa Police (BSAP), was the local Tsetse Fly Ranger.] Thatched huts, one at each end of the clearing, would serve as office and quarter-master's store.

In his book *Missionary Travels*, Dr David Livingstone described the tsetse fly, which feeds on the blood of humans and animals:

[It is] not much larger than the common house fly [whose] peculiar buzz when once heard can never be forgotten by the traveller. It is well known that the bite of this poisonous insect is certain death to the ox, horse, and dog. The animal does not die at once. It is usually a case of wasting, emaciation, purging—then death.[2]

Since Livingstone's time, research has shown that the tsetse fly carries the parasite trypanosome brucei, which it transmits through its bite. In humans, this causes 'sleeping sickness', a progressive disease beginning with fever, headache, chills, anaemia, and joint pains, and progressing to lethargy, drowsiness, and death, as it attacks the central nervous system. In animals, the disease is called Nagana, which has similar clinical features.

On the morning of 1 September 1958, journalists from the *Gwelo Times* and the *Bulawayo Chronicle* arrived to take photographs of our departure.[3] They reported:

A large crowd of parents and friends gathered at Gwelo's municipal offices to watch the mayor Mr J. C. Cannon, give his official blessing to the departing convoy. Toughening up—for the boys—began at once. Perched like tick birds [oxpeckers or egrets, which peck the ticks off the backs of animals] on a lorry load of blanket rolls, they rumbled down to the Low Veld through a day of blistering heat.

At 11.50 a.m., we arrived at Fort Victoria (founded by the Pioneers in 1891 and named after Queen Victoria), having travelled 113 miles. At 3.30 p.m., we reached the Birchenough Bridge. It spans the Sabi River and was named after Sir Henry Birchenough, one-time President of the BSAC.

According to Major Blowers, who kept a diary of events, the road 'after turn-off at Taganda River, became very corrugated'. At 5 p.m., he reported, 'Dusk falling'. At 6.20 p.m., we reached the Rupisi camp, having travelled a total of 263 miles.

Very good supper of stew, bread, jam and tea. Lads do not eat very heartily, probably exhausted from a very hot and dusty journey. They have, however, made plenty of noise in the bath.

This was a reference to Rupisi's naturally occurring hot springs, which fed into three specially constructed bathing pools. On arrival, we schoolboys, having sweltered in the heat for hour after hour, simply threw off all our clothes and dived naked into the waters, much to the disapproval of the local residents, who quickly made for the exits. That night, too, was not without incident, as Major Blowers indicated:

> We must have disturbed a nest of scorpions around the large Baobab under which we camped, as no less than eight were destroyed, the lads chasing them around and across the beds.

Next day we rose early, and after a breakfast of porridge and fried sausage, left Rupisi in convoy. At 11.20 a.m., we arrived at the Tsetse Fly HQ and had tea with Mr Jenke and his wife in their charming home overlooking the deep gorge of the Sabi valley.

For the final 18 miles of the journey the roads were reported as being 'very bad indeed.' Finally, we reached our destination and were greeted by the loud cheers and grinning faces of the advance party—the Que Que contingent under Mr J. F. Elsworth (hydrobiology) and Mr A. S. Bartholomew (geology).

A tarpaulin was suspended beneath a kaffir orange tree. This would serve as the kitchen and dining area. The staff would sleep under another tarpaulin, 'whilst the lads settled in under trees around about, some under tarpaulins and others without'. Mosquito nets were obligatory: this being the Low Veld and an area 'noted for bad malaria and blackwater'. This was a reference to an extreme and deadly form of malaria, where the destruction of red blood cells by the malarial parasite is so great that the urine actually turns black with degraded blood products: However, 'although mosquitoes were plentiful, prophylaxis proved adequate, the suppressant used being the drug Aralen in full doses, commencing before leaving, during the stay, and after return. No cases occurred'.

Although Major Blowers reported that 'by 8.30 p.m. camp dead [i.e. everyone asleep],' this was not strictly true. I had not long been asleep when I was woken by a commotion, caused by Cobus (short for Jacobus), an Afrikaner member of our party who, unbeknown to anybody, had chosen to wander off along the riverbank with his torch. Now, here he was, shocked and shaken, having suddenly come face to face with some hippopotamuses—notoriously irritable and unpredictable creatures, which feed at night, and if disturbed often attack without warning.

Since our arrival, the major had tried, without success, to contact the British South Africa Police on his radio (although he was able to pick up Rhodesian Broadcasting Corporation broadcasts from Salisbury, and other broadcasts from Mozambique and from the Union of South Africa).

Robin McGowan and I were chosen to accompany Major Blowers on a 3-mile reconnaissance of the area. From two natives, we discovered that the indigenous people here were descended from the Shangaan tribe (of Zulu origin). Although they spoke both Chilaranga and Chishangaan, the Major was able to communicate with them in Chizezuru. Dr Deuchar would later report that the Shangaans 'showed typical [signs of] hypoproteinaemia, their diet consisting almost entirely of small grains, meat being limited to fish and rodents caught in the native traps'.

After lunch, Mr Jenke arrived with some useful maps, and arranged for a local young Shangaan called Isaac, to be seconded to the expedition as interpreter. Mr Jenke stayed overnight, enjoying brandy and coffee with the leaders before retiring. 'All under nets tonight, as a mossie or two around last night.'

> The following morning Mr Jenke took two of our leaders in his boat upstream to the gorge, to view the Chibirabra Falls. Pot shots at crocodiles who show themselves. One has his tail tickled (.22 rifle). Tramp back to boat and hear shot, and hear that Parvess [O.V. Parvess, pupil of Guinea Fowl School] has shot a croc. with [a] 7mm [rifle] and it lies on the bank. John [Jenke] goes up to pool and with assistance gets crocodile aboard—was shot just behind the eye.

The sequel to this story was as follows: Parvess and his companions decided to drag the lifeless body of the crocodile from the boat back to our camp. He then lifted its front portion up onto a wooden crate. However, just as he crouched down beside it to take its photograph, the creature suddenly reared up and snapped its jaws, giving him the shock of his life. Although the croc was long since dead, this jerk was its final, convulsive movement.

Next day, we pupils were divided into groups. The geologists and botanists were driven off in the Land Rover; the ornithologists remained in the vicinity of the camp; and the surveyors and hydrobiologists (of whom I was one) were taken by lorry to the rapids.

BOYS SEEK A FABLED SABI DOOR

Sunday Mail Correspondent

Gwelo, Saturday.

A PARTY of 25 school-boys and their adult leaders leave Gwelo on Monday morning to search for the fabled stone door ruin in the lower Sabi area —and, if time permits, for the legendary wharves of an ancient port on the Sabi.

If they find the stone door ruin they will be the first Europeans to do so as there is no known record of a white man having seen it.

The ruin is said to be on one of a line of three low hills through which the road from the Lundi-Sabi junction to the Hippo mine passes.

Boys seek Sabi Door.

We hydrobiologists made tables of the relative distribution of the various aquatic species: mayflies, waterbugs, beetles, whirligigs, and so forth, which were to be found in the Gorge above the Chibirira Falls, as compared with the Flood Plane and Isolated Pools. Nevertheless, I confess that I would have preferred to have been with the ornithologists, who were having a much more exciting time:

[However, on a visit to Lake Tembahatu] a large expanse of swamp which was nearly dry, with almost impenetrable reeds 8 to 10 feet high [we saw] a very large bird like a stork, with a wing span of at least 8 feet. We also heard hippo snorts in the reeds; though we did not see any. [Words taken from my own diary, and possibly somewhat of an exaggeration!]

That evening, we tucked into a hearty meal; Mr Darwin, the quartermaster, reported:

… the amount of food available proved to be in excess of requirements. This was due mainly to the unexpected, but welcome, supply of freshly killed game, provided by the Tsetse Fly Ranger's hunters, in return for small gifts of tobacco and cigarettes from the quartermaster's store. In this we were fortunate, because John Jenke's hunters were only averaging about two buck each month, most of the game having been shot out under Tsetse Control operations. Two or three dozen guinea fowl [shot, ironically, by the ornithologists] helped to give variety to meat dishes. Apart from a few dubious eggs and some small chickens, suffering from malnutrition, the local natives had no food for sale.

Mr Magness' attempt to discover the whereabouts of a fabled ruin led him into an extraordinary adventure, as he proceeded to explain:

I first heard the story of the Stone Door Ruin from Mr R. B. Anderson, at that time Mining Commissioner in Gwelo. Legend has it that it is a Zimbabwe-type ruin [i.e. built in the same architectural style as that of the country's former capital, Great Zimbabwe] and that it has a door, on the inside of which is a carving of a man. 'It might be found,' said Mr Anderson, 'on one of a line of three *koppies* which straddled the road from the Lundi-Sabi junction to the old Hippo Mine'. Furthermore it was 'within a few miles of the river.'

Mr Janke, however, informed us that the road to which Mr Anderson had referred ran deep into Portuguese territory; access to which was forbidden without prior permission.

Mr Magness then decided to question the local Chief Mahenye, but could not make himself understood. Even when he showed the Chief a £1 note, on which was depicted an etching of Great Zimbabwe, it conveyed nothing to him. However, the Chief was able to understand that 'we were searching for the home of the ancients' and he agreed to take Mr Magness and two other leaders to that place, along with our indispensable interpreter, Isaac.

Having met the Chief before dawn next day, Mr Magness reported as follows:

We travelled by jeep several miles into thick acacia forest and at a signal from the Chief we stopped. He led us along a footpath for a few hundred yards, and then, without warning, left the path and plunged into the forest. We walked in single file in a straight line, with the newly risen sun on the back of our necks, but what guided the Chief I do not know. Occasionally he stopped and looked around as though taking his bearings. Once, he fingered the time-browned scar of a broken sapling. The forest floor was an undisturbed carpet of leaves, but he never seemed in any doubt about his destination. At last, with the atmosphere growing more and more eerie, we heard voices. This was a shock, for we thought there was no other person within miles, but the Chief led us out into a clearing where we found three men, whom Isaac later identified as brothers of the Chief. They were busily engaged in sweeping up the leaves with broken boughs.

The clearing itself was roughly 30 yards in diameter and dominated by a single ancient tree in its centre. It was surrounded by what seemed to be a solid wall of matted vegetation. We guessed, before Isaac told us, that it was the burial ground of the Mahenye chiefs. We gazed around in genuine awe. Then Isaac murmured a request. The Chief wanted a cigarette. We were all of us non-smokers, but by a stroke of fortune I had in my shirt pocket a packet of tobacco. I handed it over. The Chief opened it and immediately handed a generous pinch to one of his brothers. What followed next amazed us. The man took a large leaf, placed the tobacco upon it and walking to the great tree, he dropped on one knee and laid the leaf at its foot. We watched, fascinated, as he clapped his hands and then spoke to the tree. When he had finished he collected his bough and went back to his sweeping.

Having returned to camp, Mr Magness asked Isaac to translate what Chief Mahenye had said in his address to the spirits of his forebears. The answer reveals the chief's confusion as to the purpose of Mr Magness's visit to him:

Oh Mahenye, these are not men of our kind. These are white men. We do not know why they are here. They say that they wish to see the place where our people lived long ago. And that is why they are here.

Continued Mr Magness:

It was plain from the demeanour of Chief Mahenye and his brothers that they held the place in great respect. It had been the site of the kraal of the first Mahenye, and so was truly the old home of his people. He visits the place only twice a year, once to clear the place up, sweep and scuttle, as his brothers were doing at that time, and then a second time when the rains are due, to give beer and grain to the spirits of the departed chiefs and ask their permission to start planting.

There was little else to relate, except that the Chief had asked Isaac to inform us that we were probably the only white men ever to see this sacred spot. As for the Stone Door Ruin, said Mr Magness, 'perhaps one day we will be back again with a permit to cross the border, but at the moment the lost ruin is still lost.'

Major Blowers also kept a diary, in which he recorded as follows:

Friday 5 September, evening. Usual forgathering and early supper. Three meats, guinea fowl, kudu and beef; tomato, carrot and potato: really got the lads beat this time!

Saturday 6, 3 p.m. Fishing from rock. Doc [Dr Deuchar] takes three bream and I one—under half pound. Mike [a pupil] fishing elsewhere pulls three small bream after earlier taking one tiger [fish]: very pleasant. On way back unsuccessful crack at guinea fowl roosting in tree.

Sunday 7, 3 p.m. [Watched 35-mm] film of dancing at kraal and chief in his robes. Poor standard of dancing and poor garb; most of able-bodied men are away—plenty of women but men only old and decrepit or young. Also pictures of bangle-maker—aluminium wire hammered out and fitted to leg.

The women referred to above were attired in colourful hats and dresses, typical of the style worn back in Britain some years previously. In fact, it was distinctly likely that Britain was, indeed, the place from where the clothes had originated, having been collected and sent out to Africa by various charitable organisations.

Monday 8, 10 a.m. To Mahenye's kraal for more filming of more women stamping, winnowing and grinding corn in usual manner. Beer drinking, working up for homecoming of Sabi men from the mines. [A reference to the fact that many of the village men worked in the nearby coal mines.]

Finally, on Wednesday 10 September, we struck camp. The expedition had been not only most enjoyable, but also a great success from the scientific point of view— if not from the viewpoint of wildlife conservation. For example, within a 2-mile radius of our camp the ornithologists had shot, and stuffed, no less than forty-eight varieties of bird, including Madagascar bee-eater, hadeda ibis, and white-flanked flycatcher (a species normally found only in Kenya). In addition, another fifty-seven varieties were sighted, including black-headed oriole, brown-headed parrot, and scarlet-chested sunbird.

Regretfully, Dr Deucher, in his medical report, had an item of sad news to relate:

The only casualty was the African cook who had an obvious liver complaint, to which he succumbed shortly after the trip; a hepatoma [tumour] was found to be present. A few of the local Africans sought medical attention including one [for a] TB [tuberculous] knee.[4]

Further Topics of Interest: 'Judy'

My father quickly adopted the habit of listening to the news on the radio, just as he had done in England; though, this time, it was broadcast not by the BBC, but by the Rhodesian Broadcasting Corporation. Now, instead of hearing about crime, road accidents in the fog, strikes, or party politics, it was 'Three ivory poachers were apprehended today in the Wankie Game Reserve'; 'A bush fire has destroyed a kraal on the outskirts of Selukwe'; or 'An African women was taken by a crocodile on the banks of the Limpopo River'. What risks the black women were forced to take simply in order to do their washing. Finally, 'Several spectators were fined for drunkenness at last Saturday's football match between Fort Victoria and Umtali'. Some things are the same the world over.

A topic of considerable interest was the proposed new dam to be built at Kariba Gorge on the Zambesi river, below the Victoria Falls. This would be the largest dam and hydroelectric scheme in Africa, and the *Rhodesia Herald* newspaper gave regular reports on its progress. One headline, for example, read, 'World Bank lends £28,600,000 at 5pc [interest]', and continued:

> The World Bank in Washington made a loan of 80,000,000 dollars to the Federal Power Board to help pay for the first stage of development of the Kariba power scheme.

As for those animals which had been trapped by rising waters during the flooding of the Kariba valley, Mr Dick Rogers, a member of the Executive Committee of the [animal] Hunters' Association, declared that his organization backed, to the hilt, the Southern Rhodesian Game Department's plans for rescuing them.[1] And the *Rhodesia Herald* reported that anaesthetic-carrying darts would probably be used on those larger animals which had to be moved to safety. Another article, headed, 'Animals' Dunkirk: Hunters Back Game Department', revealed that not only animals, but also human beings, were at risk.

The surging waters of the Zambesi river have drowned at least 15 Africans, destroyed a school, inundated villages and a power station, and halted work on part of the Kariba Dam operations, where the water is already 8ft above the coffer dam [constructed to hold the waters back while the main dam was being built]. Giant pumps will be brought into action to save the concrete shell [of the coffer dam] from being shattered by the weight of water.

Sadly, several further accidents occurred during the construction of the dam. Workmen involved in the operation lost their footing on the catwalks; fell into the concrete below, and were entombed. Nevertheless, the main wall of the dam 'was completed ahead of schedule on 21 June 1959'. However, almost 100 lives had been lost in the process.[2]

When my father announced that he was to fly to Northern Rhodesia to give a course of lectures on 'slow-learning children', my mother said she was afraid to be left alone in the bungalow with Jane and me in a strange country. Her fear was made greater by the fact that we had recently had what might be described as a burglary, which we discovered one morning when we awoke to find a trail of banana skins leading from the lounge to the kitchen. Whether a man or a beast was responsible, we never did discover. To my mother, the answer to the problem was a simple one: she would like a dog, and preferably a large one.

We visited the local pound near Gwelo, and made ourselves known to the manager Mr Appel, who invited us into the yard to see what was available. 'I'm not going in there with all those hundreds of animals!' said my mother nervously. 'You'll be all right,' said my father. 'Come on!' and with further reassurances from Mr Appel, we all trooped in, as dogs of various shapes and sizes raced around in all directions. How did one make one's choice?

Suddenly, from a distance, a large, smooth-haired, sandy-coloured creature came bounding towards us at speed, and made straight for my mother. 'Keep still. She won't hurt,' said Mr Appel. We held our breath, and before my mother knew it, two large paws were placed on her shoulders, and a long, wet, velvety nose was thrust lovingly into her face. From that moment the two of them were inseparable, so much so that she used to say, 'I don't want to die and go to heaven unless "Judy" is there with me.' Judy was the name we gave the dog.

Judy was a mongrel, mainly of the 'Rhodesian Ridgeback' variety, as was born out by the characteristic raised ridge of fur that ran down the centre of her back. Her colouring was typical of the breed—her coat being a lustrous golden brown. Ridgebacks are fearless, and were originally bred for the express purpose of hunting (in packs) lions, which preyed on cattle.

Right from the start, it was obvious that Judy was devoted to my mother, whom she followed everywhere. When my mother got up from her chair and went from the lounge to the kitchen to make a coffee, Judy followed. She even followed mother to the bathroom and tried to get into the bath with her. It was mother's habit to feed

Judy and our cat, Toots, in the kitchen at the same time. Toots generally finished first and pestered Judy, by going over to her bowl and pushing her nose into it. This stretched the poor dog's patience to the limit, until finally, with her forehead wrinkled into an exasperated frown, she would pick her bowl up in her teeth and carry it across the kitchen and onto the *stoep*, there to finish her meal in peace. She was capable of performing this feat, not only with a bowl of meat, but also with one of milk, without spilling a drop.

To exercise Judy, I would take her across the road and hold her up on her hind legs so that she could see over the top of the tall grass. This enabled her to catch a glimpse of the springbok, which were invariably to be seen grazing in the far distance. I would point her long nose in that direction, and whisper, 'There girl, see!' Suddenly, she would tense her body, prick up her ears, give me a brief glance which said, 'Thanks for your help,' and go bounding off. However, when she had closed the distance between herself and her quarry to a few hundred yards, the buck would sniff the air, and then amble nonchalantly away. Then, as Judy drew nearer, they would take off in great bounds—a Morris Minor against an Aston Martin—and she would come slinking back, crouch at my feet and look at me mournfully, as if to say, 'Sorry. I'll try to do better next time.'

Every month, it was the custom among the black employees of Glengarry School, all of whom were male, to pool their savings and send whoever was at the top of the list into Gwelo to buy himself a gleaming brand-new bicycle. As there were eleven black members of staff in total, this could mean a one-year wait.

Although Judy was an excellent guard dog, she had a bad habit, presumably learned from her previous owner, of barking at black people and pursuing them in a most aggressive manner. To see one pass by on a bicycle was a temptation that she simply could not resist, and try as we might, we could not break her of this habit.

One day, Judy saw M'Johnny, the venerable, white-haired post-boy, cycling majestically by on his way to Glengarry School (to which post was delivered; whereas for individual bungalows, it had to be collected from the post office in Gwelo). Off went Judy like a rocket, snapping at his heels. M'Johnny, however, had the answer. Without slowing down, or even seeming to turn a hair, he reached for the knobkerrie (wooden stick with bulbous head, used as a club), which he carried fastened to his handlebars with two metal clips. At the sight of this, Judy fled, tail down, knowing that she had been outmanoeuvred. M'Johnny wielded his knobkerrie majestically and to great effect. The more intelligent dogs quickly learned their lesson. Those less so could be identified by the egg-shaped swellings on their heads.

One day, before we went to Gwelo to do our shopping, my father summoned Timot: 'Timot, I have a request to make of you,' he said gravely. 'Eh, *baas*?' 'Will you please let Judy out at about midday for her to do her toilet?' Timot looked at Judy apprehensively. She, in turn, stared back at him, growling, and turning up her lips to display two rows of gleaming white teeth. 'Yes, *baas*, Timot let dog out, no trouble!' However, we arrived home later that afternoon to find trouble a-plenty. There was a foul smell in the house and Judy was looking sheepish. Clearly, she had had an 'accident'. Moreover, Timot was nowhere to be seen. 'Timot!' cried my father. He duly appeared, his head hung down in shame as Judy snarled at him from a distance. '*Maninge indaba*,' said my father (meaning: 'This is a very serious matter.') 'Why, pray, did you not let Judy out?' There was a pregnant pause. How would Timot extricate himself from this situation, I wondered? '*Baas*, your dog Judy, she is too cheeky!' replied Timot, shuffling nervously from one foot to another, at which we all fell about laughing.

Apart from this unfortunate flaw in her character, Judy, in other respects, was a loveable, faithful creature and I have an enduring picture, in my mind's eye, of her lying on her blanket in the back garden, on grass greened by the first rains after nine months of drought. She loved the shade of the 'flamboyant' (which, in early summer, was covered in glorious sprays of scarlet flowers) beneath which was a flower border where purple African violets bloomed.

The Matopos: Great Zimbabwe

The search for the fabled Stone Door Ruin, which we had undertaken in our expedition to the Sabi river, had wetted my appetite for Rhodesian history. This was further reinforced by a visit we made to the Matopos National Park, situated in Matabeleland, to the south of Bulawayo. The Park encompasses a great range of granite hills, extending over 1,250 square miles and topped by enormous boulders and groups of balancing rocks, overlooking wooded valleys. From Gwelo, this had entailed a motorcar journey of about 100 miles.

Recognising the beauty of the area, Cecil Rhodes had been instrumental in the construction of a special 8-mile length of railway line from Bulawayo, in order that the people of that city 'may enjoy the glory of the Matopos from Saturday to Monday' (i.e. at the weekends).[1] It was in the Matopos that many of the most dramatic events of Southern Rhodesia's history were played out, as will shortly be seen. It is also the place where Rhodes chose to be buried.

In the Matopos, there are many caves, some decorated with paintings, which allow for an insight into the earliest inhabitants—the Bushmen—those of this particular region being known as the San. A race of nomadic hunters, it was only natural for them to depict themselves, in their paintings, in the midst of the profusion of wildlife with which they were surrounded.

Bushmen are small in stature with a wrinkled appearance, excellent eyesight, and a fondness for art and song. Their language abounds with 'clicking' noises. Caves were their preferred habitat, but they also lived in primitive huts made of branches. Their skill as trackers is legendary.

The so-called 'Rock Art' of Southern Rhodesia originated in the 1st millennium AD; painting in Matabeleland reaching its peak in the sixteenth and seventeenth centuries.[2] In the Bambata Cave were portraits of steenbok, eland, and tsessebe antelope, and warthogs and mongooses. All were in a colour, which had retained its vividness for many centuries: the paint being made from pigments of iron oxide, ochres, and clays, which the Bushmen mixed with animal fat and the exudate of the cactus plant, euphorbia. In

Great Zimbabwe. (*Photo: Gillian Lewis*)

the Nswatugi cave, which extends deep into the hillside, there were equally fine colour portraits of human beings (presumably depictions of the Bushmen themselves), together with kudu antelope, giraffe, and elephant. In the Silozwane Cave, to which we and our fellow visitors gained access via a steep path, we saw fishes, birds, and a snake.

What became of the Bushmen? Their fate was decided by a people who came originally from the Niger/Congo region of Central Africa, known as the 'Bantu', who shared a common language (of which there are over 200 sub-groups), and who had learnt to cultivate crops and use metals to make tools. From the seventeenth to the nineteenth century, the Bantu extended their sphere of influence by colonizing the whole of Central and southern Africa.[3]

On the arrival of the Bantu, the Bushmen, now regarded as aliens in their own land, were simply murdered or driven into the western deserts. There were currently said to be no Bushmen remaining in Rhodesia (and less than 1,000–2,000 in South West Africa).

Our visit to the Matopos answered a question that had exercised me for some time. This stemmed from the constant arguments at school as to which race of peoples had arrived in Southern Rhodesia first. To the minds of some of my fellow pupils, whoever had arrived first could reasonably claim ownership of the land—provided that those arrivals were their forebears, of course! The same view was held by the blacks. However, we had now proved, beyond all doubt, that it was neither the whites nor the blacks who had arrived first: the original native inhabitants being, according to the available evidence, the San Bushmen.

I was interested to know, in particular, from whence Timot had originated, and when I asked him, he replied proudly, 'Timot, he Karanga.' Whereupon, I researched in the library and discovered that the Karanga people came south from the Niger/Congo region as part of the Bantu migration to settle in the eastern part of Bechuanaland, and in the adjacent area of (what was now) south-western Southern Rhodesia. Their language is similar to Shona, indicating a common ancestry (other Karanga pressed on and colonised the region between the Limpopo and Vaal rivers, later known as the 'Transvaal'; or crossed the Vaal into what later became the 'Orange Free State').

The next piece of the jigsaw that was Southern Rhodesia's history was filled in for us following our visit to Rhodesia's most famous and enigmatic monument: the Great Zimbabwe Ruins, which lay 70 miles to the south-east of Gwelo near Fort Victoria; the word 'Zimbabwe' deriving from the Shona 'dzimba dza mabwe', meaning 'houses of stone'.

The first white person to discover Great Zimbabwe was Rhodesian trader, hunter, and explorer Adam Renders (born in Germany in 1822) of Zoutpansberg (later Northern Transvaal), in the winter of 1867.[4] The ruins cover an area of 3 square miles within which are three enclosures, the walls of which are built of blocks of local granite, hand-trimmed and put together without the necessity of mortar (in many instances, naturally occurring granite boulders have been incorporated into the stone walls).

Having learnt that we planned to visit Great Zimbabwe, Jane asked if she could invite Mikey van der Pole, one of her Afrikaner classmates at school to accompany us. Unlike the normal Afrikaner who was tall, rugged, and large-boned, Mikey was small, wiry, and, as we soon discovered, extremely agile. Soon after our arrival, there he was, halfway up Zimbabwe's conical tower, clinging on to its dry stone walls with his fingertips and toes of his bare feet, as we watched him with a mixture of horror and admiration.

The conical tower, which is of solid construction, is 33 feet in height and measures 16 feet in diameter at the base, tapering to 6½ feet at the top. Adjacent to it is a smaller tower. Both towers are contained within the Great Enclosure, described as the largest, single ancient structure south of the Sahara Desert. Its perimeter wall measures 827 feet in length, and is 30 feet in height. It is estimated that in the region of a million granite blocks were used in its construction.

In the adjoining valley are the so-called Valley Enclosures; the presence of numerous dagga floors within indicating the former site of fifty or so households. Many more dagga floors exist outside the enclosures, indicating that, in its heyday, the population of the Great Zimbabwe Complex may have exceeded 10,000.

Jane and Mikey van der Pole
at Great Zimbabwe, Chris in
background.

Towering above is the Hill Complex, situated on a steep-sided granite mound that
rises 260 feet above the surrounding plain. This consists of a number of enclosures,
interconnected by narrow, stone-built passages. The largest of these is the Western
Enclosure with a perimeter wall 26 feet in height and with a thickness of 16 feet.
On the eastern side of the Hill Complex is another enclosure containing a number
of man-made stone platforms. It should be pointed out that Great Zimbabwe is
not unique, in that more than 150 smaller stone-walled complexes occur, not only
throughout the Zimbabwe Plateau, but also, as far afield as Botswana, Northern
Transvaal, and Mozambique.

Who built Zimbabwe, when, and for what purpose? Although many of its
archaeological remains have been destroyed in the past by careless excavation,
artefacts discovered on site include iron and decorated copper-bronze axes and
spears, an iron gong, copper wire, ivory, gold objects, and a large variety of pottery.
There are also imported goods such as glass beads, Chinese celadon of the Ming
dynasty, and Persian faience (an indication that Great Zimbabwe was linked to
trading centres along the East African coast).[5]

By far the most exciting archaeological finds, however, were those made by Willie Posselt of Middelburg (Cape Province) who described a trip taken by him and his brother in 1889:

> ... decided to take our second trading-and-hunting trip to Mashonaland and visit the [Zimbabwe] ruins. [There,] In an enclosure which served as a cattle kraal, I saw four soap stones (soapstone—or steatite, a malleable metamorphic rock), each carved in the image of a bird and facing towards the east. Each one, including its plinth, had been hewn out of a solid block of stone and measured four foot six inches in height; and each was set firmly into the ground. There was also a stone shaped like a mill-stone and [measuring] about eighteen inches in diameter, with a number of figures carved on the border. I selected the best specimen of the four bird stones—the beaks of the remainder being damaged, and decided to dig it out.[6]

Posselt believed that this, the finest of the bird specimens, later found its way to Cape Town Museum.

> The remaining stone birds were removed by Mr and Mrs James Theodor Bent who came from England in 1891, to begin a two-month period of archaeological excavations at Zimbabwe Ruins.[7]

Eight carved birds were discovered in total: each one being unique. However, although they are all bird-like in shape, they also possess features characteristic of human beings. The one found in the Western Enclosure, for example, has lips rather than a beak, and all have four or five toes, rather than three talons. What is the significance of these carvings?

> In Shona belief, birds are messengers, and eagles, such as the batalur [a large eagle that inhabits tree and Bush savannah throughout Southern Africa], brings word from the ancestors. Ancestral spirits in turn are supposed to provide help and bring success. Soaring like an eagle to heaven, the spirits of former leaders were supposed to intercede with god over national problems such as rains. Since each bird is unique, they probably represented specific leaders (i.e. of the Shona people). The (sitting) birds from the Hill Ruin probably signified the ancestral spirits of ... women. The (standing) birds of course, symbolized the spirits of important male leaders. Somewhat surprisingly, similar carved birds have not been found in other Zimbabwe culture settlements.[8]

As to the origin of Great Zimbabwe, author Lorna Edwards points out that 'few of the world's great ruins have aroused such heated controversy, or have given rise to such divergent theories of when, why and by whom they were built. Skeletal remains were conspicuously absent'.

Roger Summers, in *Ancient Ruins and Vanished Civilizations of Southern Africa*, suggested that the chevron-patterned wall of the temple and conical tower could have been the work of the ancestors of the Lemba (Bantu speaking peoples of Jewish origin, who migrated to the Yemen in about the year 7 BC), 'who were the actual traders sent inland by the Arab merchants on the coast'.[9]

It has been suggested that Great Zimbabwe was once the capital of an important region in the heart of what became Southern Rhodesia. Evidence that this may indeed have been the case, comes from the writings of the writer and traveller al-Masudi of Baghdad:

> [al-Masudi] journeyed by sea from the Persian Gulf down the east coast of Africa to Sofala in modern Mozambique, in or about AD 922, [and] clearly recorded the existence of a substantial trade in gold and ivory, which was shipped from Sofala to Oman, and thence to China and India. The king of this state bore sublime titles such as 'Son of the Great Master, the God of the Earth and Sky'.

According to authors Roland Oliver and J. D. Fage:

> It is highly probable that Masudi was referring to a state whose rulers were later responsible for the earliest stages of stone building at Great Zimbabwe, currently attributed by archaeologists, on the basis of carbon-dating, to approximately the 11th century.[10]

Author Bettina Schmidt stated that when, towards the end of the fifteenth century, the State of Great Zimbabwe declined, so, one of its former tributary states, Munhumutapa (whose ruler was called the Mutapa) in the northwest, became pre-eminent. Said she:

> In the first phase [*c*. 1500–1624] Portuguese traders and missionaries infiltrated the Munhumutapa state. In the second phase, during the early seventeenth century, the Portuguese were able to gain control over the gold and ivory trade, making the Mutapa a Portuguese puppet. In the third phase, after approximately 1663, the recently enthroned Mutapa regained control and the Portuguese were forced to withdraw from the territory. But thereafter, internal strife and fissions at the periphery of the early state led to its political decline.[11]

To summarise, it seems reasonable to assume that Great Zimbabwe was constructed by the people of Munhumutapa in about the eleventh century. Whether it functioned as a military fort or a place of worship, or both, or simply as a trading post, remains a matter for conjecture. And where are the famous soapstone birds of Zimbabwe today? Five of the eight are currently in the custody of Zimbabwe's Department of National Museums and Monuments.

Advent of the Missionaries

In 1859, almost a century prior to our voyage to South Africa on the Union-Castle Line vessel RMS *Edinburgh Castle*, missionary the Reverend John Smith Moffat and his wife, Emily, left England for Cape Town, sailing aboard RMS *Norman* of the Union (later Union-Castle) Line; the journey took some forty-two days. Their objective was to travel to Matabeleland (later a province of Southern Rhodesia), there, with the consent of its ruler, the self-styled 'King' Mzilikazi (or Moselekatze, who was, in fact, not of royal blood), to establish a mission station.

Mzilikazi's story was as follows: Appointed as a commander in the Zulu army in 1817, he had failed, following a successful raiding expedition, to send tribute to Tshaka, Zulu King (of the territory which subsequently became known as Natal). This being the case, Tshaka sent a punitive expedition to destroy him, whereupon Mzilikazi fled across the Drakensberg Mountains and began to lay waste the land later known as the Orange Free State and the Transvaal.

> This great black king [Moselekatze] had settled in a district north of the Vaal river. He was an absolute terror in the land, for his warriors scoured the country, burned the native villages, speared even the women, and cast their helpless infants to the flames. He became known as the 'Monarch of Blood and Tears,' for he wiped out every living creature he came across.[1]

Having arrived at Cape Town, the Moffats were greeted by John's parents, the Reverend Robert Moffat (born in Scotland in 1795) of the London Missionary Society and his wife, Mary.

Since 1816, the Reverend Robert had worked as a missionary in southern Africa, and in 1825, he had established a mission station at Kuruman in the British Protectorate of Bechuanaland. In 1829, Mzilikazi arranged for his warriors to bring the Reverend Robert to meet him. The meeting was an amicable one. The King nicknamed his visitor 'Moshete', and told him that he was puzzled as to 'how

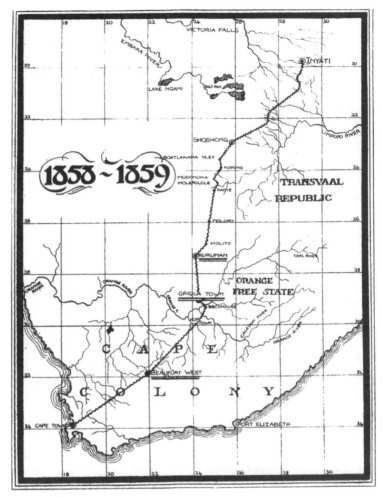

Drawn by Vivien Smart

Map Showing Route Taken
By the Missionaries
From Capetown to Inyati

The route taken by the missionaries.

the small front wheels of the [i.e. Robert's] wagons could keep up with the big hind wheels'.[2]

In 1835, the Reverend Robert paid another visit to Mzilikazi from Kuruman. As a result of this meeting, Umnobate, the King's chief counsellor, entered into a treaty with the governor of the Cape Colony the following year, whereby Mzilikazi agreed 'to be a faithful friend and ally ... to protect all white men who may visit his country, and to defend and treat in a friendly manner all missionaries ... [and] to defend and assist all travellers or traders...'[3]

Early in 1838, however, after battles with both Boers and Zulus, Mzilikazi was once again forced to flee: this time northwards cross the Limpopo river. He and his followers now settled near the Bembesi river, in what later became Southern Rhodesia. According to Mrs Phoebe Taylor of Kuruman, the inhabitants of that region, the Shona, instead of meekly submitting to Mzilikazi, offered him some resistance. Said she:

> The bow and arrow was the principal weapon used by the Mashonas, but they also had some muzzle-loading rifles traded from us [i.e. the British]. Arrows and spears were all poisoned, and many of the Matabele [i.e. Mzilikazi's warriors] who were hit probably died later on.[4]

Nonetheless, for the Shona, it was all in vain, and they were either murdered, enslaved, or driven into the hills. Mzilikazi now established his capital at Inyati and called his newly-won territory Matabeleland. His followers became known as the Matabele (or Ndebele) meaning literally, 'those who disappear'—that is, are able to blend easily into the bush.

In 1854, the Reverend Robert again visited Mzilikazi, the King having been taken ill. This involved him in a 700-mile journey—the distance from Kuruman to Matabeleland. Three years later, Robert visited the King yet again to request permission to open a mission station in his country. Mzilikazi agreed, provided that this was done either by Robert himself or by his son, John. As Robert felt unable to leave the Kuruman Mission, it was decided that John should make the necessary arrangements with the King. This, then, was the purpose of the Reverend John Moffat's visit to southern Africa in the year 1859.

The party of missionaries and their wives who would now travel north from Cape Town included John Moffat and his wife, Emily; John's father, the Reverend Robert Moffat, who had agreed to accompany his son in order to introduce him to his longstanding friend King Mzilikazi, and his wife, Mary; and the Reverend Thomas M. Thomas and the Reverend William Sykes and their wives. Also present was Mary, the Reverend Robert's eldest daughter, who, in 1845, had married the famous missionary and explorer Dr David Livingstone (who had been sent to South Africa in 1841 by the London Missionary Society).[5] Mary and David Livingstone had recently sailed from England, but the former had taken ill during the crossing so David had travelled northwards to the Zambesi without her.

The journey of the missionaries and their entourage northwards was, of course, very different from the one which we had undertaken—there being no railway from Cape Town in 1859 (in fact, its construction was commenced on 31 March of that very year). Their only means of transport was by ox-wagon, and it would take them five long months.[6] John Moffat's wife, Emily, kept a diary of events. It revealed that the journey was not only arduous, but highly dangerous for both humans and animals alike. When entering a tsetse-fly belt for example, 'the cattle had to be taken to drink under cover of darkness when the fly would be asleep'.[7] Another hazard of the journey was 'rinderpest', described as 'a most infectious disease, attacking animals which chew the cud, such as cows and oxen. The sickness is like a fever and affects the animals' digestion, making them weak and listless all through their bodies.[8] [Rinderpest is in fact caused by a virus.]'

Emily Moffat's impressions of the Karoo Desert, encountered during the early stages of the journey were much the same as ours:

> ... a bare, howling wilderness where everything was scarce except sand and dust. [Here] the poor oxen, dragging the heavy wagons and obtaining nothing to feed on, gave way [i.e. succumbed] one after another.[9]

Finally, they arrived at the Kuruman Mission Station, where the party was joined by the Reverend Thomas Helmore and the Reverend Roger Price and their wives, whose intention was to bring a mission to the Makololo, a tribe living near to the Zambesi. From Kuruman, the missionaries would set off for Matabeleland—a journey that entailed crossing the Limpopo river. Lilian Emily Stuttaford of the Orange Free State described a trek, made from Vredefort in that province to Bulawayo, more than three decades later in 1895:

> At Limpopo river ... which was also known as Crocodile river, because it was infested with crocodiles ... one of our best oxen got stuck in the mud at the far bank. Harry, aged 18, who acted as driver all the way, did not know about the crocodiles. He had been a powerful swimmer in England, so he swam over to the ox, extricated it and brought it safely back. When an old transport rider who happened to be with us at the time heard what Harry had done, he literally turned pale.[10]

I recall, on our journey northwards from the Cape, crossing the Limpopo river at Beit Bridge and gazing down at the mighty Limpopo river from the comfort of our railway carriage. What a contrast, with what those nineteenth-century missionaries such as the Moffats and others were obliged to endure.

On their arrival in Matabeleland in that year of 1859, the missionaries, having decided to dispense with their oxen that were currently suffering from lung sickness rather than risk them infecting any of the King's cattle, found themselves in some difficulty. Mzilikazi, King of the Matabele, came to the rescue by announcing that his warriors would assist in hauling the missionaries' wagons for them. However, the arrival of the Matabele warriors was an unnerving experience. The Reverend John Moffat's wife Emily, described the event:

> [The] poor naked fellows ... staring at us and all we do ... the men all stood in a long row, shields and spears in their hands. In turn several rushed out from their places and danced, or rather, leapt about with great zest and struck their shields on the ground,

some only once or twice, others eight or nine times, corresponding with the number of men killed by the actor.... Shouts of applause from the onlookers. This was truly awful. Every sound went to my heart as the funeral knell of a fellow creature.[11]

Finally, John Moffat and his party were conducted safely to Mzilikazi's residence at Inyati.

The King's *kraal* consisted of royal residences where he and his wives lived; scores of other huts, which housed his peoples; and enclosures for his 4,000 or so cattle. He also possessed several wagons, which served as royal coaches.

Mzilikazi received them very kindly and promised to treat them well. He [also] sent the ladies a large piece of cooked meat. [As for his warriors they] considered it a great honour to have been sent by their king to bring the first missionaries.[12]

Behind the scenes, however, the King was in a dilemma. It was said by some that the missionaries had been 'sent up-country to spy out the land before other white people would follow. Also [that they were] wizards, who would catch a crocodile, make a charm with its liver and bewitch Mzilikazi'. The outcome was that the missionaries endured 'five wretched weeks of suspense' before the King agreed to provide a suitable site at Inyati for the mission station. It was 26 December 1859.[13] This would be the first white settlement in that country.

There was a sad footnote to the story, for in their endeavours, the missionaries had paid a heavy price. By 1862, three years after the party had set out from Cape Town, there had been no less than ten deaths among them, including Mrs Moffat's baby, Unwin, and Mrs Annie Thomas and her daughter, Annie (junior), aged two months. The death of the Reverend Helmore and his wife and two children was alleged to have been due to poisoning by slave dealers who 'realized how the missionaries would oppose their business of dealing in slaves'.[14] Mary Livingstone herself was among their number, for having met with her husband at Shupanga on the Zambesi on 1 February 1862, she contracted malarial fever and died on 27 April.

It has to be said that the success of the missionaries was somewhat limited, Mrs Caroline Kirkham (of the Inyati Mission Station) declaring that her father, the Reverend Thomas Kirkham, during several years spent in Matabeleland, had succeeded in baptising 'only nine natives. The whole spirit of the Matabele was against Christianity,' she said.[15]

Following the death of Mzilikazi in 1868, the Reverend Kirkham attended the inauguration (in 1870) of his successor: his son, Lobengula (who also styled himself 'King'). After this, according to Zulu precedent, a new capital was built at Gubulawayo.[16]

With the passage of time, many more mission stations were established in what became known as Southern Rhodesia. Here, black children were fed, clothed, and received their religious instruction (usually Roman Catholic) and education.

15

A Latter-Day Missionary

Our Standard Vanguard, with my father at the wheel, juddered and jolted along the dusty strip road, across the featureless miles of 'veld'. We were *en route* from Gwelo to visit friends who worked at the local asbestos mine. My father calculated that it was best to drive at 80 or so miles per hour over roads such as the one we were travelling on—made of dirt, and pitted and eroded after the rainy season—so as to skim over the deeper ruts, and he was now putting his theory into practice, despite my mother's protestations.

Most black people had the presence of mind as soon as they heard the roar of his engine to head for the safety of the grassy verge. On this occasion, however, an elderly black cyclist whom my father was catching up with fast, failed to take evasive action until the very last moment (perhaps he was deaf), before wobbling into the bank and falling from his bicycle into the long grass. My father stopped the car, whereupon we expected that he would get out, offer the frightened man his apologies, and help him to his feet. Far from it! Instead, to our embarrassment, he wound down the window and enquired pompously in his best 'pigeon English', 'And what do you think you are playing at?'

We had not long resumed our journey when, suddenly, out of the bush, emerged a party of black people, mostly women, carrying on their heads such varied items as a car radiator, cooking pots and pans, bundles of clothes, a radiogram, and miscellaneous cardboard boxes, which, it transpired, contained Holy Bibles and hymn books. In the lead was the tall, thin, bedraggled figure of a white man, aged about thirty, attired in a threadbare, khaki shirt and shorts, and wearing a dog collar. He flagged us down and asked if we would give him a lift to nearby Fort Victoria, where he told us he was due to officiate at a church wedding. He had no car, as it was currently being repaired (the reason for this we would discover later).

As this involved only a modest detour, my father agreed. My mother and Jane, who were sitting in the rear seats, moved up, whereupon the reverend gentleman got in and sat beside them, having first placed his briefcase and some jam jars containing coins in the boot. This represented a collection, mostly of threepenny coins ('*tickies*') that, he said, had been generously donated by his black parishioners (his parish being situated way out in the bush). When my mother asked him what his name was, he chuckled. 'It's Salmon, actually. I'm afraid it's rather fishy!'

We duly delivered the Reverend Salmon to the church: a red-brick building in Fort Victoria's main street. Some of the surrounding buildings, he told us, were over sixty years old, and had been constructed by members of the Pioneer Column. He was late already, so taking his briefcase and the jam jars with him, he dashed into the vestry to put on his vestments. Then, just as quickly, he rushed out again to enquire of my father if he possessed a stud for his collar, and of me as to whether he might borrow my Boy Scout belt to hold up the grey flannels that he had changed into. I obliged, but my father could not. My mother, however, being more resourceful, produced a paper clip, which proved adequate for the purpose. The Reverend Salmon then asked if we would kindly return after the service and give him a lift to Mashaba, which, as it happened, was also our destination. He said he had friends there who would accommodate him. Again, we agreed to his request. Having time on our hands, we visited the local shops and purchased some provisions with which to make a picnic. Then we paid a visit to the park, where we consumed our cool drinks and cold chicken—which by now had warmed up in the heat.

Having returned to the church, we collected the Reverend Salmon and continued on our journey. We realised that we had reached our destination of Mashaba, when huge mounds of a greyish-white powdery substance, 50 feet or more in height, came into view. This was asbestos, Rhodesia's second most important mineral export after gold; the mines here, and at Belingwe, were among the largest in the world. In fact, everything in the vicinity of the mine—vegetation, buildings, and vehicles alike—was covered in dust, and we wondered, in retrospect, how many people's health had been ruined by working in such an environment. Having delivered the Reverend Salmon to his destination, we arrived, now several hours late, at the home of our hosts-to-be: the Kincaid-Smiths, members of a venerable Rhodesian family. However, this was not the last we were to hear of our friend, the Reverend Salmon.

Having returned home, my mother recalled that she had recently read in the *Rhodesia Herald* an account of a road accident where the name 'Salmon' was mentioned. It concerned the Governor-General of Southern Rhodesia Lord Dalhousie and his family, who had just returned from a visit to the United Kingdom. They were travelling along in their chauffeur-driven Bentley motorcar from Salisbury Airport when they collided with a small car; the driver being none other than the Reverend Salmon.

The accident had come about in this way. When driving on the strip roads (which were laid down in the 1930s: the very first being the one that linked our home town of Gwelo to nearby Selukwe), the convention was that when two vehicles approached one another, both moved over, each leaving their two off-side wheels on the nearside tarmacadam strip. On that fateful day, the Reverend Salmon had been travelling behind a lorry, which, as he approached it, had pulled over in the prescribed manner. Assuming that the lorry driver intended that he should pass—whereas the driver had, in fact, done so because an oncoming vehicle was approaching—he pulled out and in the ensuing cloud of dust, ran head-on into the Governor-General's car. Lord Dalhousie's daughter, allegedly, lost several front teeth due to the impact, and His Lordship was obliged to send his Bentley all the way back to England for repairs. As for the Reverend Salmon's vehicle, it was adjudged to be a write-off.

Although I have never subscribed to any particular religion, my parents decided that I should attend Confirmation classes, after which I was duly Confirmed in Gwelo's Church of St Cuthbert by James Hughes, Archbishop of Central Africa, who, despite signing himself 'James Matabele', was a white man.

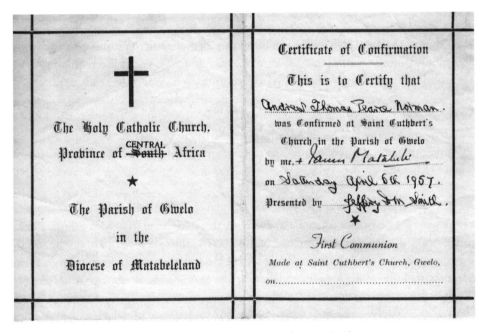

Andrew's Certificate of Confirmation by Archbishop of Central Africa.

The Victoria Falls:
Dr David Livingstone

Our sojourn at Victoria Falls followed immediately after our visit to Wankie Game Reserve, and entailed a journey of about 100 miles in our faithful Standard Vanguard motorcar. Once again, I draw upon my diary to rekindle the atmosphere of those heady days.

Monday 26 August 1957
We went up many hills, and suddenly, over the top of one, we looked right down, about 3 miles and saw lots and lots of white mist rising in the valley. It was the spray from the Victoria Falls.

As we drew nearer, we became aware of a sound like distant thunder, above that of the car's engine. At a distance of 1 mile, the very earth beneath the wheels of the car shook.

We were accommodated at the Main Rest Camp in a furnished, thatched, 2-bedroomed hut with living room/kitchen. Each bed was fitted with a mosquito net, and also the window, so even when it was open, mosquitoes and other insects could not gain entry.

Tuesday 27 August 1957
In the car park there are lots of baboons. They are a menace, because when a person leaves the car door open, the baboons jump in, ransack everything, and sometimes carry things off. Nevertheless, we enjoyed watching them.

Notices all around warned us to keep the car's windows and doors tightly closed against the troops of baboons, but even when this was done, they were liable to wrench open car doors, or tear holes in their fabric hoods as if they were made of paper. These powerful and unpredictable creatures are quite capable of attacking any small child or pet dog left unattended. Offer them bread or a biscuit, and they take it with a leap and an ungracious snatch. Fail to do so, and they register their disapproval by snarling, and baring their teeth in a fit of fury, to which they are prone.

We decided to walk down to the rain forest. We followed the path to the Devil's Cataract. It was one huge mass of water which dropped a long way down to the water below. From here we could see the top part of Cataract Island.

As I stood watching, awestruck on a rocky ledge, I felt light-headed, as if I was being drawn, inexorably, downwards by some supernatural force. It was then, that my ever-vigilant father noticed the trance-like state which this vision had induced in me and, taking my arm, lead me gently away to safety.

The Victoria Falls are over a mile in width. On the very edge of the precipice are several rocky outcrops, the largest of which are Livingstone Island and Cataract Island. These outcrops serve to divide the water into six separate waterfalls, named (from west to east) Devils Cataract; Main Falls; Horseshoe Falls; Rainbow Falls; Arm Chair Falls; and Eastern Cataract. The height of its component waterfalls varies, the lowest being the Devils Cataract at about 200 feet, and the highest, the Rainbow Falls at about 350 feet.

The waters cascade downwards into the (first) gorge, and exit through the Boiling Pot—a narrow cleft in the rocks about 160 yards wide and 160 yards long. The river then turns sharply westwards into a 1.3-mile-long (second) gorge, at the commencement of which it is traversed by the Falls Bridge. Then, at the Silent Pool, it turns sharply to eastwards into the 1.2-mile-long (third) gorge. On a more practical note, located in the 3rd gorge is a hydro-electric power station, which was commissioned in 1936.

The Falls Bridge.

The Zambesi river reaches its peak volume in mid-April, when columns of spray rise to over 1,500 feet and are visible from 80 miles away. Now, four months later, the river had subsided somewhat, as had the spray which would otherwise have obscured the view, so that the 'awe inspiring chasms ... bounded by the tracery of the myriad waterfalls' that we had read about could clearly be seen.[1]

On account of the perpetual mist, the whole area atop the far side of the 1st gorge into which the water cascades, is a tropical rain forest, in contrast to the otherwise arid surroundings.

> We walked on through the rain forest, and occasional bursts of condensed spray burst over us. In the rain forest are lots of palm trees, creepers [*Ficus ingens*—a strangling creeper that eventually kills the tree which supports it], and monkey ropes [*Rhoicissus tomentosa*—a plant of the grape family whose rope-like stems may reach to the tops of trees]. Further on, we saw a bit of Livingstone Island, and many rainbows all around.

Immediately above the Falls, the Zambesi boasts an archipelago of islands, some of which are situated only a few hundred yards from where the water plunges down over the edge. One of these is called Livingstone Island, where stands a tree (marked by a ring of stones) on which Dr Livingstone carved his initials.

It was from the island which bears his name that Scottish missionary and explorer Dr David Livingstone, first caught sight of the Falls on 16 November 1855; he being the first white man ever to do so. Livingstone's Makalolo (Nyasa) interpreters knew the Falls as Mosi-oa-Tunya ('the Smoke that Thunders'). Livingstone however, named them after Queen Victoria.

> Finally, to Danger Point [on the western cliff top, above the Boiling Pot], from where we looked across to the Eastern Cataract and went down into the gorge. It was very exciting.

From here, we could see the Victoria Falls Bridge, completed in 1905, which carried a railway, road, and walkway. In accordance with the wishes of Cecil Rhodes, the bridge was sited in a position where the windows of the trains which passed over it would be washed with spray. 420 feet above low water in the river below, the bridge at the time of its construction, was the highest in the world.

> Wednesday 28 August 1957
> Jane and I walked down to the Falls. As we stopped at Devil's Cataract, I looked to the left end of the falls and saw the large statue of David Livingstone overlooking it. He had a Bible in one hand and a walking stick in the other.

So now, with Dr Livingstone's statue towering above me, and the mighty Victoria Falls before my eyes, the pages of my boyhood magazine the *Eagle*, which I had read

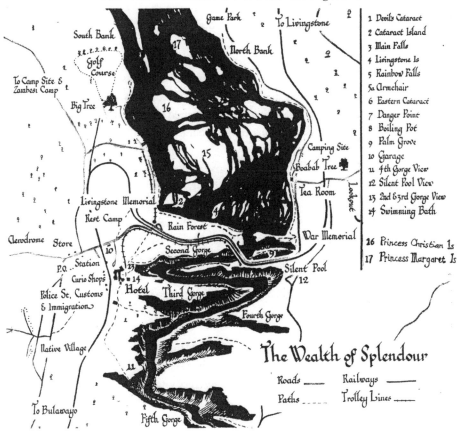

Game Park
To Livingstone
South Bank
North Bank
17
Golf Course
To Camp Site &
Zambesi Camp
Big Tree
16
25
Camping Site
Boabab Tree
Tea Room
Lookout
Livingstone Memorial
Rest Camp
Rain Forest
War Memorial
Aerodrome
Store
Second Gorge
P.O. Station
Curio Shops
14
Silent Pool
12
Police St. Customs
& Immigration
Hotel
Third Gorge
Fourth Gorge
Native Village
11
To Bulawayo
Fifth Gorge

1 Devils Cataract
2 Cataract Island
3 Main Falls
4 Livingstone Is
5 Rainbow Falls
5a Armchair
6 Eastern Cataract
7 Danger Point
8 Boiling Pot
9 Palm Grove
10 Garage
11 4th Gorge View
12 Silent Pool View
13 2nd &3rd Gorge View
14 Swimming Bath

16 Princess Christian Is
17 Princess Margaret Is

The Wealth of Splendour

Roads —— Railways ——
Paths ---- Trolley Lines —·—

Above: Zambesi River and Victoria Falls—'The Wealth of Splendour'.

Right: Victoria Falls, statue of David Livingstone.

so avidly back in Lichfield, and the images on my boyhood stamp collection, had veritably come to life!

> In the afternoon, we decided to go on a drive to the lookouts and the Silent Pool. We went to the first look out, up a big hill. On the top was a baobab tree, with some steps and a platform near the top. We climbed this and had a good view of the Falls, and some gorges of the surrounding countryside.

On Thursday 29 August 1957, we drove over the Falls Bridge, which marks the border between Southern and Northern Rhodesia, and followed the Zambesi to the town of Livingstone, 6 miles away. At the Rhodes and Livingstone Museum we saw 'weapons of the various tribes, works done by an African artist, information on how Livingstone discovered the Falls, and how he measured them, and manuscripts taken from his diary'.

On Friday 30 August 1957, my parents embarked on 'a 10/- (10 shilling) trip up the Zambesi', while Jane and I 'went down to the curio shop. There were many skins there, silver jackal, squirrel coats, springbok skins etc. I decided to make a little collection of ivory animals'.

When my parents returned, they said they had travelled by motor launch around King George VI Island, a mile or so upstream, but seen nothing 'except a crocodile's nose sticking out of the water'. Nearer to the terrifying edge, however, canoe trips were advertised from the west bank to Cataract Island, and from the east bank to Livingstone Island—something which was only possible after the rainy season when there was a sufficient depth of water. This was not for the faint-hearted. Apart from the inherent danger of being swept over the Falls, the river was teeming with hippo, which can capsize a small boat, and crocodiles ready to take advantage of such an eventuality! Also, the river teemed with ferocious tiger fish, which attacked even our pocket handkerchiefs when we dipped them into the water, and would, we were assured, strip our fingers to the bone within seconds, were we unwise enough to give them the chance!

Later, we sat on the banks of the Zambesi, above the Falls, which was perhaps even more frightening than actually looking over the edge, as the black oarsmen paddled their little boats between the islands, seemingly oblivious to the colossal forces which were at work nearby.

A black man approached and asked if we would care to be photographed with his 'bush-baby', which he kept on a chain. A nocturnal animal related to the lemur, this creature has large ears and including its long tail, measures about 30 inches in length. In the wild, it lives on a diet of flower petals, honey and insects. It is particularly adept at preying on pheasants and guinea-fowl: creeping up and overpowering them as they sleep. Jane was the first to volunteer, but no sooner had she taken the friendly-looking creature in her arms, than it gave her a nasty bite on the lip. She screamed. Its black owner apologized profusely, and we hurried away to find the

Christ Church Primary School, Lichfield, Staffordshire. Andrew middle row, third from left.

Postage stamps of Southern Rhodesia.

UNION-CASTLE LINE

Southampton Water

LIST OF PASSENGERS
R.M.S. "EDINBURGH CASTLE"
From Southampton 19th April, 1956

RMS *Edinburgh Castle*,
passenger list.

RMS *Edinburgh Castle*,
Jean and Chris.

R.M.S. "EDINBURGH CASTLE"   CHILDREN

Tea

Cereals
Savoury Fish Cakes, Tomato Sauce
Fried Potatoes
Minced Lamb with Green Peas

Eggs:
Boiled   Parsley Omelette
COLD
Smoked Ham   Galantine Ivoire
Plain & Dressed Salads

SWEETS:
Peaches with Cream
Wonder Cake   Chocolate Roll

White and Brown Bread and Butter
Tea   Hot or Cold Milk   Cocoa
Fruit

Tuesday, 24th April, 1956

UNION-CASTLE LINE

RMS *Edinburgh Castle*, menu.

RMS *Edinburgh Castle*, Andrew and Jane in fancy dress.

7 RMS *Edinburgh Castle*, Andrew's certificate for 'Crossing the Line'.

Above: Jane, Jean, and Andrew, with Standard 'Vanguard' at home at Thornhill.

Below: Jean with pupils of Glengarry School.

Left: Adias and M'Johnny, employees of Glengarry School.

Below: Glengarry School, acacia trees in foreground.

Right: Andrew and Jane in school uniform.

Below: Gwelo: the Town Hall.

Above left: Gwelo, Jean beneath poinsettia tree.

Above right: Jane at the McGill's farm.

Below: Street vendor, Bulawayo. (*Photo: Gillian Lewis*)

Above: Chris, Andrew, Jane, and Jean on picnic at Ferny Creek.

Below: Gwelo: parade to celebrate Her Majesty the Queen's official birthday.

Above: Railway and strip road from Gwelo to Selukwe. (*Photo: Gillian Lewis*)

Below: Elephants coming to drink at salt pan. (*Photo: Joan Dudley*)

Above: A friendly hippo, being reared on a bottle, its parents having been shot by poachers. (*Photo: Joan Dudley*)

Below: The bush fire.

Above: Elephants bathing at Kariba. (*Photo: Pat Bennett*)

Below: Andrew and Judy.

Above: Bushman paintings, Bohwe Cave, Matopos. (*Photo: Gillian Lewis*)

Below: 'World's View', Matopos.

Above: Victoria Falls. (*Photo: Gillian Lewis*)

Below: Matopos: Shangani Monument and grave of Cecil Rhodes.

Above: Chibero Agricultural College for Blacks. (*Photo: Gillian Lewis*)

Below: On the farm, blacks at their lessons. (*Photo: Gillian Lewis*)

Above: Fletcher High School for Blacks, Gwelo. (*Photo: Gillian Lewis*)

Below: Robert Mugabe. (*Photo: The Zimbabwean*)

Jane on the banks of the
Zambesi River.

local doctor who administered an anti-tetanus booster injection and prescribed a
course of antibiotics.

'Scenes so lovely must have been gazed upon by angels in their flight,' wrote Dr
Livingstone of the Falls. However, there was a down side, for on Saturday 31 August
1957 at the local cemetery, we came across the graves of forty or so early white
settlers: men, women, and children (some in their infancy) who had perished at the
turn of the century. Some graves bore not only the name of the deceased, but also
the cause of death—most commonly, malaria induced blackwater fever.

Cecil John Rhodes: Gold!

Throughout the Federation of Rhodesia and Nyasaland, the first Monday in July was celebrated as a national holiday called 'Rhodes and Founders Day' (or as the locals irreverently called it, 'Rhodes and Scroungers'), and in a ceremony attended by the Governor-General, the Union Jack was raised on the flagpole at the Pioneer Memorial in Salisbury.

Cecil John Rhodes was born at Bishop's Stortford in Hertfordshire, England, on 5 July 1853. Suffering from tuberculosis of the lungs, he was sent, at the age of seventeen, to Natal, where his brother was already an established farmer. This was in the hope that the clean air would improve his health. It did, and when diamonds were discovered at Kimberley in the Orange Free State, Rhodes moved to that place and prospered by setting up in business: selling excavating equipment and water pumps to the newly-opened mines. This led in 1880 to his founding the De Beers Diamond Mining Company. Rhodes was also active in politics, and in 1884, he was appointed to the Cabinet of the Cape Colony and served, for a time, as its Treasurer.

When gold was discovered on the 'Rand' (Witwatersrand, an area south of Johannesburg in the Transvaal), Rhodes invested in these fields, and in 1887, he established the Goldfields of South Africa Company.

According to the aforementioned missionary the Reverend T. M. Thomas, in the early 1860s, the English hunter and explorer Henry Hartley 'heard a rumour from the Boers of the Transvaal that there were ancient gold workings in Mzilikazi's kingdom at Tati [near the border with Bechuanaland] and elsewhere'.

Accordingly, and with an eye to exploiting these gold fields, Hartley obtained permission from Mzilikazi to hunt big game in Matabeleland and Mashonaland. In this, he 'was clever enough to get the advice of Karl Mauch, a German mineralogist who knew his job, and this gentleman accompanied Hartley on his next hunting trip in Mzilikazi's kingdom'.

Hartley's careful preparation paid off because it was while he was hunting that he noticed 'groups of ancient workings', although 'personally he had little knowledge of gold-bearing rocks.' The Reverend Thomas gave 1866 as the date for the 're-discovery of the northern goldfields', and 1867 for the rediscovery of those at Tati.[1]

The first application to exploit the goldfields at Tati was made by a Mr Jan Viljoen of the Transvaal Republic, to whom the King replied: 'Mzilikazi grants the request of the white people to come and dig out the stone of gold … but he [the King] cannot sell any part of his dominions, nor can he grant permission to any other nation to come to live, nor even to settle down for any length of time in the land'.

Soon afterwards, numerous gold seekers from Britain and her colonies, and from Germany and Australia, 'poured into the country'.[2]

In 1888, Rhodes, ever ambitious, sent Charles Rudd, his business partner at Kimberley, and two others northwards to the country soon to bear his name. Here, they met with Mzilikazi's successor, Lobengula, King of the Matabele, at his capital Gubulawayo, with the purpose of securing rights to the mineral deposits in his territory, which they knew from Hartley's and Mauch's explorations to be present.

Rudd offered Lobengula 1,000 rifles, 10,000 bullets, a steamboat with guns for use on the Zambesi, and £1,200 a year for himself and his heirs. In return, the latter signed away the mineral rights to his 'kingdom, principalities and dominions'. The signed document, known as the 'Rudd Concession', was at once sent to Rhodes in South Africa; he presented it to the British Government.

Rhodes's problems were not yet over; prior to this, Edward Lippert, a German Jew, had visited Lobengula and also obtained from the King mineral concessions in Matabeleland of considerable value. Rhodes was therefore obliged to negotiate with Lippert in order to be able to exploit his own mining interests in that region. This resulted, in 1889, in the signing of the 'Lippert Concession', which allowed would-be British settlers to acquire land rights from the indigenous people. In practice, the British South Africa Company (BSAC) purchased concessions from the British Crown and then sold them to the settlers; the revenue accruing to the Crown (the black owners of the land received nothing).

Rhodes now contracted twenty-three-year-old Major Frank Johnson, formerly of the Bechuanaland Border Police, to organise a pioneer column that would occupy Mashonaland. This would consist of 200 hired adventurers (none of them over the age of twenty-five years), together with 117 wagons, to be guided by the famous elephant hunter Frederick Courteney Selous. As the BSAC was unable to afford the expense of maintaining an occupation force, Jameson agreed that the prospective volunteer settlers should each be rewarded with '3,000 morgen' (about 6,300 acres of land), together with 'twenty gold claims'.[3] The document, signed to this effect by Jameson, was known as the 'Victorian Agreement'.

The column duly set off from Macloutsie, Bechuanaland, on 28 June 1890. On 11 July, it crossed the Tuli river to begin a 400-mile trek into Mashonaland (as Lobengula had not given his unequivocal consent to European occupation, Frank Johnson and his Pioneer Column gave the King's territory of Matabeleland a wide berth). Eleven weeks later (a makeshift road having been built along which miners and farmers would follow), the Union flag was raised to a twenty-one-gun salute on a hill near Mount Hampden in Mashonaland. It became known first as Fort Salisbury and later, simply as Salisbury.

The next problem to arise occurred when the fabled gold (which German geologist Karl Mauch, had said was present) was nowhere to be found. This caused many of the pioneers, who had each been promised a farm and fifteen gold claims, to give up in disgust and return to Johannesburg—shares in the BSAC having slumped from £3.15s to 12s. Others chose to remain, and so became the first white settlers to colonise Mashonaland.

The 'gold rush' having proved to be a huge disappointment, the Pioneers turned their attention to the land: each claiming the 6,300 acres, which had been promised to him by Rhodes. Those who followed in the footsteps of the Pioneers were treated even more generously because Jameson awarded vast tracts of land 'to wealthy individuals and syndicates, on condition that they spend agreed sums of money on the development of their property'. Rhodes's aides were also extremely well rewarded. For example, Major Sir John Willoughby, the Pioneer Column's second in command, 'was awarded no fewer than 600,000 acres, after promising to spend £50,000 on its development'.[4] 'Willoughby's Consolidated Company eventually accumulated 1.3 million acres. Rhodes's surveyor-general, on taking up his post, was 'awarded' 640,000 acres'.

The missionaries also benefited, acquiring almost one-third of a million acres. This meant that within ten years, a total of about 16 million acres (or one-sixth of the land area of what subsequently became Southern Rhodesia) had been appropriated by whites.[5]

The potential of gold and precious metals as a vehicle for investment was what had sparked Cecil Rhodes's interest in the land that would one day bear his name, Rhodesia. Although the gold prospectors of the 1890s had failed to find it, there was, in fact, gold aplenty. This was by virtue of the Great Dyke: a chain of hills bisecting the country and stretching some 320 miles from north-east to south-west—created some 700 million years ago by an upheaval in the Earth's crust. In the upheaval, rocks rich in minerals were brought to the surface. The names of the goldfields that subsequently sprung up on either side of the Great Dyke linger romantically in the memory: 'Globe and Phoenix', 'Fred and Redwing', 'Cam and Motor', 'Muriel', and 'Golden Valley'. Little did I think that I would ever get my hands on a sizeable chunk of this highly valuable metal, yet this proved to be the case—albeit only temporarily. It came about thus.

At a meeting of the Gwelo Philatelic Society, my mother, a keen stamp collector, met a couple called Alf and Joanna Bott. Of cockney descent, Alf, in a former life, had been manager of a London omnibus company and had emigrated to Rhodesia in the early part of the century. He was now personnel manager at the Connemara Mine north of Gwelo on the Que Que road—in charge, as he said, of 'hiring and firing the boys' (by which he meant the black employees).

Despite the passing of the years, Alf had retained his cockney accent and also his cockney wit. His wife, an Afrikaner originally from South Africa, was an equally charming woman. The Botts were not only entertaining, but also most hospitable to us, and we became frequent visitors to their cottage, which nestled between two enormous mounds of waste from the mine.

The Botts's garden was like a little piece of England, with verdant lawn and roses of both bush and climbing variety—an effect that they could only achieve by keeping their water-sprinkler on at all times.

The Botts loved animals, and taught members of the local black community to bring to them for treatment any injured creatures that they happened to come across. Alf even performed minor operations—there being no veterinary surgeon for miles around. For example, when it became necessary to dock the tail of their puppy, he performed the task himself; first numbing the aforesaid tail by freezing it with ice from the refrigerator. There were cats everywhere (we counted seventeen, but there may well have been more), each one having its own cushion on which Joanna had thoughtfully embroidered its name. Every evening she stood outside the back door and banged a tin plate with a metal spoon to summon them for their supper. We were also shown a collection of tiny tortoises which the Botts had bred. They told us about their pet duck 'Donald', which was so domesticated that he lived more in the house than out of it. When Donald went missing, Alf suspected that one of the 'boys' had stolen it for the pot.

Once a week, Joanna held a sewing class for the wives of the black mineworkers. She remarked upon their patience because unlike European women, she said, they were not hampered by the constraints of time. In the evenings, when we visited, we would all sit out on their stoep, watching fireflies which darted about like tiny stars, while the adults drank their 'sundowners'.

Meanwhile, down at the mine, a tunnel had recently collapsed, leaving a huge, gaping hole the size of a football pitch. The mishap occurred when a huge excavator was brought to the site. Unfortunately, its great weight had proved too much and when the mine collapsed the excavator completely disappeared, never to be seen again. Fortunately, there had been no loss of life.

Alf showed us how the crude ore was brought up from below on a conveyor belt to be sorted by the black workers, whose task it was to look out for the metallic glint that signified the presence of gold. The ore was then pulverised between two gigantic and thunderously noisy metal rollers, after which it was treated with acid and centrifuged; the metal residue being pushed to the outside of a great, circular, rotating disc. However, the highlight of our visit was when Alf took us into his office, opened the safe, and lifted out a shiny gold ingot the size of a house-building brick. This represented one month's production, and when he handed it to me, it was all I could do to bear its weight.

My mother drooled over Alf's stamp collection. He had been a collector for years, restricting himself to Britain and the Commonwealth. Knowing we too had an interest, he always gave Jane and me a little packet of 'swaps' before we left.

It was everyone's dream to make his fortune by discovering gold or precious metals, or precious stones. This dream was fulfilled for prospectors Laurence Contat and Cornelius Oosthuizen in October 1956.

High-quality emeralds, the first to be found in Southern Rhodesia, have been discovered in the Belingwe Native Reserve. [Situated near Shabani, at the south eastern end of the Great Dyke] An area of 500 square miles has been fenced by the Government and placed under police protection. To protect the world emerald market, export of these and several other precious stones has been prohibited, except under special licence. A Salisbury jeweller told the *Rhodesia Herald* yesterday that first-class emeralds would command a higher price than similar quality diamonds.[5]

The Matabele War and Rebellion

On a second visit to the Matopos, we came across a monument on the banks of the Shangani river. It measured 33 feet in height and was made of granite blocks hewn from a neighbouring kopje. Designed by Scottish sculptor John Tweed, and dedicated by Bishop Gaul of Mashonaland in 1904, it carried the simple inscription: 'To Brave Men'. It was, in fact, a commemoration of a battle between Pioneer forces and the Matabele, which had come about in the following way.

Since their arrival in 1838, King Mzilikazi and his Matabele warriors had enslaved the indigenous Shona, who now became their subject people. As for King Lobengula, who succeeded on the death of his father in 1868, he was capable of displaying hideous cruelty to those who crossed him. This was born out by Mrs Caroline Kirkham (*née* Thomas) of the Inyati Mission, who stated that the King had 'killed his own brother because the people grew very fond of this brother, and Loben [gula] was afraid they might make him king. He also killed his sister Nini. It was reported that Nini had got very fond of one of the white men and wanted to marry him; so Loben ordered her to be choked to death'.

Mrs Kirkam also quoted Francis Thompson, one of the three men who had negotiated the Rudd Concession:

One of Loben's subjects had dared to taste the king's beer as it was being carried to his kraal. First, Loben made his warriors cut off the man's nose because it had smelt the king's beer; next his lips, because they had tasted the king's beer; then his ears, because he had heard that no-one must taste the king's beer en route [to the King], and had disobeyed. Then the Matabele were ordered to hide his eyes, because they had seen the king's beer. This was done by skinning his forehead and allowing the skin to hang down. Lastly, he was thrashed.[1]

By all accounts, the pleasure that the Matabele derived from torturing animals was equally depraved and sickening.

Although Lobengula continued Mzilikazi's tradition of treating the missionaries with consideration, with the presence in Mashonaland of Cecil Rhodes's pioneers, tensions grew between them, the Matabele, and the Shona. Matters came to a head when the Matabele attacked Mashona *kraals* near Fort Victoria in July 1893, killing the inhabitants and looting their possessions. Following this, Jameson ordered the Matabele *impis* (armed bodies of men) to vacate the area. They refused, and on 3 October 1893, the so-called Matabele War began.

Jameson now raised three attacking columns: one under the command of Major Patrick Forbes in Salisbury; the second under Major Allan Wilson (born in Ross-shire, Scotland) at Fort Victoria, and the third under Colonel Goold Adams and Commandant Pieter Raaf in Bechuanaland. Various attacks by the Matabele were repulsed with the use of Maxim machine guns, and on 4 November 1893, the first two columns marched, side by side, into Chief Lobengula's capital at Gubulawayo, where all they found was the burning remains of the Royal *Kraal*, and two Europeans whose lives had been spared at the King's command. Lobengula, together with his remaining *impis*, had fled towards the Zambesi river.

Knowing that there would be no peace while Lobengula remained at large, Jameson ordered Major Forbes (who had successfully wrested the area around Umtali, known as 'Manicaland', from the Portuguese three years previously) and his column to set off in pursuit. The rainy season was imminent, and there was no time to lose. In the event, the weather would act in Forbes's favour. From then on, the story, as far as it is known, is told by Major Walter H. Howard, who witnessed some of the events at first hand:

A strong Column under Major Forbes … reached Shiloh [a deserted mission station] during a terrible thunderstorm on the 23 November [1893], where they were joined by Captain Napier with rations and reinforcements.

Very little progress was made during the next four days owing to rain affecting the wagon transport. On the 28th Major Forbes decided to send back to Inyati all the wagons and dismounted men, continuing the pursuit with mounted men only. This force consisted of approximately 158 officers and men, with two Maxims [machine guns] on galloping carriages. Pack horses carried extra ammunition and ten days' half-rations for the Column. Progress now was more rapid and satisfactory. Two days' forced marching found us hot on the scent. Every precaution was taken against surprise. There were front and rear guards and flankers [presumably people guarding the flanks].

The Patrol reached the Shangani river about 4.30 p.m. on the 3 December. Just before we halted we passed through very large *scherms* [screens made of thorn branches and tree trunks to protect against attacks by wild animals] that had been hurriedly vacated—cooking pots still on the fires and things lying scattered about all over the place and large herds of cattle could be seen being hurried away up the river. Yet still no sign of the king; only the fresh spoor of his wagon which we were told had crossed the river the day before.

The Column laagered up close to the river about 5 p.m. Major Wilson was sent on with twelve men to follow up the spoor, with orders to return at dark.

The word '*laager*' derives from the Cape Dutch word '*lager*', meaning a camp. To the early Dutch settlers, or '*Vortrekkers*', however, the word referred to a defensive fortification, created by drawing wagons closely into a circle and closing the intervening spaces with impenetrable thorn bushes. Women, children, and cattle were placed in the centre; the men defending the position against the enemy, while the women loaded their guns and tended the wounded.

Although all were tired out, some sat up late that night to hear what news Wilson would bring back. About 11 p.m., Captain Napier returned with two men from Major Wilson. They reported that Wilson had passed through several *scherms* occupied by natives and one that had a high fence was pointed out as that of the king. After a long discussion, Major Forbes decided to send Captain Barrow with twenty men and some food to reinforce Wilson, with a message that we would follow next morning as soon as it was light enough to see.

To this end, the main body of the column set off, but was forced to turn back, having been ambushed by black attackers. Before it (the column) had beaten off the attack, however, Major Howard stated ominously: 'we heard the firing from Wilson's party die down, then re-open and again die down'.

It was during the retirement that the column was joined by Frederick Burnham, Pearl 'Pete' Ingram, and William Gooding, who had got away from Wilson's party before the fighting became desperate. It was their opinion that they were probably the sole survivors of that party, which indeed proved to be the case. The column then retreated along the Shangani river, until it met with a relief column that included Rhodes himself and Jameson. It later transpired that Lobengula had made one final attempt at reconciliation, having the previous day 'sent in by two natives a message to Dr. Jameson, together with a gift of £1,000 or £2,000 in gold. The messengers were met by two of the flankers who took the money and kept it, sending the natives back to their king. The theft was discovered when this gold began to be put into circulation. If Lobengula's message and offering had been delivered, there would certainly have been no Allan Wilson disaster'.[2]

Rhodes requested that 'the remains of Allan Wilson and his party be brought to Malindidzimu [World's View, Matopos] from Fort Victoria and placed inside the memorial I shall put up to their memory'.

On our visit to the Matopos, my family and I inspected the monument carefully and, in particular, the panels on each of its four sides, depicting in life-size bronze relief, all the members of the ill-fated Shangani patrol who perished. Sadly, no similar memorial exists to the Matabele, who, armed mainly only with assegais, bravely faced the British guns.

Having returned home, I purchased, from a black craftsman in Gwelo market, a miniature buckskin shield impaled with two crossed wooden *assegais*. This, I hung on my bedroom wall to remind me of the great battles of yesteryear, fought between the British and the Matabele. Another reminder was a small, but beautiful bird with blue and lilac plumage, which we often caught sight of. This was the 'Mzilikazi Roller'—named after the great Zulu leader (tradition has it that no one, except the current Zulu king, may use its feathers for decoration). What became of the missionaries at Inyati?

> The Reverend and Mrs Bowen Rees had been settled at Inyati Mission Station over five years when the Matabele War broke out. It is always said that Lobengula had become very fond of them. As soon as he realised that the white settlers were arming to fight him, he kindly sent messengers to Mr Rees advising them to leave Inyati at once because he might not be able to protect 'his missionary,' as he always called Mr Bowen Rees.[3]

King Lobengula is said to have died in remote bushland near the Zambesi river on 23 January 1894. The circumstances of his death remain a mystery, but it marked the end of the so-called Matabele War. The Chartered Company (BSAC) now proceeded to destroy his capital, and cattle formerly belonging to the Matabele were shared out amongst the settlers. Bulawayo was now founded at a site a few miles distant, and here Rhodes, who had now supplanted the King, built himself an official residence. Two years later, the country was officially named 'Rhodesia' after its founder.

As for Mr and Mrs Bowen Rees, when they returned to Inyati later in 1894, it was reported that 'they got a great welcome from several Christian natives'.[4]

The Matabele Rebellion of 1896 was an event so traumatic that it was still remembered, even in the Rhodesia of the 1950s.

In January 1896, Jameson was defeated by the Boers in the ill-fated 'Jameson Raid' (an expedition against the South African Republic, which will be discussed shortly). This event not only denuded Southern Rhodesia of its troops, it also made the Matabele realise that the forces of the white man were not invincible. In March of that year, they rose in rebellion, murdering an estimated one-tenth of the white population in an orgy of violence in which the Shona were not slow to join in. The terrified inhabitants of Salisbury, Bulawayo, and other centres were therefore forced to go into '*laager*' for their own defence.

During the Matabele Rebellion, the inhabitants of our home town of Gwelo were forced to laager for a period of five months—their numbers having swollen to around 600, for every white person in the vicinity took refuge there. This included twenty-seven women, twenty-two children, many mineral prospectors (others of whom were murdered *en route*), and the soldiers of the town's garrison. Instrumental in assisting the sick and injured among Gwelo's beleaguered citizens was Mother Patrick (Mary Anne Cosgrave, born in Ireland), a nun of the Dominican Order. Having arrived in

Mashonaland via South Africa in 1881, she subsequently became matron of the Fort Salisbury hospital, which the Dominicans had established. This was followed, in 1896, by the opening of the Bulawayo Memorial Hospital, and shortly afterwards, of a new hospital at Gwelo. Mother Patrick subsequently became the first Prioress general of the Dominican Sisters in the Rhodesian colonies.

Subduing the fearsome Matabele warriors, who were expert in the use of the short, stabbing *assegai*, was no easy task, even for British Army officer Colonel Herbert Plumer, who arrived in Southern Rhodesia with reinforcements from the Cape. However, Cecil Rhodes brought the Matabele Rebellion to an end when, accompanied by three Europeans and two blacks, he walked, unarmed, into their stronghold in the Matopos Hills for an *indaba* (discussion), and persuaded the *indunas* (chiefs) to lay down their arms. An obelisk was subsequently erected in Gwelo Gardens to commemorate those who lost their lives in the Matabele Rebellion. In Mashonaland, however, the rebellion dragged on for another year; the fighting finally ending in October 1897.

The word '*indaba*' became assimilated into the vocabulary of the European settlers, which now included that of our own family. If there was a difference of opinion, someone would say, 'Let's have an *indaba* about it'. Alternatively, 'That is your *indaba*' meant 'That is your business' or 'That is your problem'.

For the victorious whites, a Legislative Assembly was established, Rhodes promising that eventually the country would be granted self-government. Meanwhile, the Native Reserves Order in Council of 1898 created areas designated specifically for black persons only, on land of mediocre quality—the whites having appropriated the most fertile portions for themselves.

Mrs Jeannie Boggie:
A Living Link with the Past

An elderly lady called Mrs Jeannie Boggie (*née* Manston, originally from Aberdeenshire in Scotland) of Craigievar Farm, Gwelo, did us the honour of inviting us to tea. Having begun her career as a journalist in Edinburgh, she had become secretly engaged in 1900 to her cousin, Major William James Boggie, when he was invalided from the Boer War. In the early 1900s, the Major purchased a tract of land on the outskirts of Gwelo, where he created a farm, 'Craigievar'. On 20 September 1917, on Major Boggie's return from the Western Front, he and Jeannie were married in Aberdeen, whereupon they set off together for Southern Rhodesia, aboard the Union Castle liner *Balmoral Castle* (then in use as a troopship).[1]

Having reached the end of her drive, which wound its way, seemingly endlessly, through the bush, we arrived at Mrs Boggie's farmhouse: a dilapidated, one-storey building with tiny windows and a corrugated iron roof. This was a prefabricated structure, which had been shipped out from England many years previously.

We noticed that the gravel turning-circle was littered with rusting cans of beans and fruit, and against the wall, an antediluvian wooden kitchen table groaned under the weight of what appeared to be cannon balls. Mrs Boggie confirmed that this was indeed the case, and that the cannon balls in question, dated from the time of the Boer War, in which her late husband the Major, had participated. The interior of the farmhouse was equally disorganised, as we were shortly to discover.

Mrs Boggie—whose skinny body was bent as the result of arthritis, but whose eyes remained keen and bright, as did her mind—lived alone in conditions of some austerity. Her hallway was piled high with copies of the *Rhodesia Herald*, going back to the days of antiquity. As we passed through the kitchen, I noticed many empty gin bottles.

She told us that, in former times, it had been her daily habit to inspect the boundaries of her farm on foot, but when she reached the age of eighty, she chose to do this the easy way—on horseback. Unfortunately, however, she had fallen and broken her arm. She was admitted to Gwelo Hospital, from where she

Mrs Boggie with 'MacGregor'.

discharged herself prematurely. Tomorrow, she told us, was her day for chopping wood and attending to broken fences. 'Do sit down,' she said, showing us into her lounge.

Her houseboy, Robert, brought in a tray of tea. 'Do you like rock cakes? These are homemade.' I bit into mine—it was aptly named. Jane failed to make any impression on hers whatsoever; so in order not to give offence, she surreptitiously put it in her pocket. Having enquired briefly about our lives, Mrs Boggie began to tell us her own remarkable story, commencing with her arrival at Gwelo's railway station as a newlywed.

> A huge farm wagon was waiting there with twelve matched red-and-white oxen. My husband, who was at heart a lover of farming, seemed to remember the names of all the oxen, and went along the line saying: '*Sa bona*, ['greetings', or 'I see you' in Zulu] Hartop; *Sa bona*, Biffel, and so on. This is your new *inkosakaas* [mistress].' So there was I, all dressed up, being introduced to twelve oxen, instead of to twelve friends.[2]

The Major had forgotten to inform his friends that he was now married!

When Major Boggie died in 1928, his widow offered his extensive collection of books to the Bulawayo Town Council, which promptly declined the offer on the grounds that they had insufficient room to house it. Over the years, Mrs Boggie herself wrote several books about her life in Africa, and every year she sent a copy of her most recent volume of poems to Her Majesty Queen Elizabeth II. In *First Steps in Civilizing Rhodesia*, she paid tribute to her late husband.

Major W. J. Boggie; buried 10 February, 1928, on Craigievar Farm, Gwelo; Pioneer of Southern Rhodesia 1894; Member of Southern Rhodesia Parliament from 1920 until his death; served in the Matabele Rebellion, the Boer War and the Great War.

She had a clock, complete with clock tower, erected in his memory and placed in the centre of Gwelo's main street, outside the Midland Hotel. But when visitors to the hotel complained about the noise it made when striking, its mechanism was removed and it fell silent.

Mrs Boggie impressed upon us how important it was for ladies in such climates as Rhodesia's to wear hats. She had always been accustomed to doing so, and this was clearly the reason why her complexion had remained youthful and fresh. Those who were less prudent risked their skins becoming shrivelled like dried tobacco leaves, with years of exposure to the merciless African sun.

Her home was something akin to a museum of natural history: the walls being hung with 'trophies'—the heads of the many unfortunate animals that had been shot by her late husband, the Major. There were also skins of various species of snake. 'I expect you are wondering what this is,' said Mrs Boggie, going over to the mantelpiece and picking up an elongated white skull. 'Actually, it's the skull of Henry. He was my favourite hunter.'

She took a loaded revolver out of the sideboard drawer, and to my father's horror, because it was pointing directly at him, began spinning the chamber. 'You can't be too careful here, out in the bush,' she said. It was her custom to keep the curtains of her living room closed, but with the sash window open. This was in order that she might poke the barrel of her shotgun through and fire it in the event of intruders (I noticed that the eucalyptus to which she referred was riddled with pellet holes, and that precious little of its bark remained). She also possessed what she called a 'pull-back-the-spring' airgun to shoot birds perched in the fruit trees. Finally, the late Major's heavy shotgun stood in the corner, for use in case of a real emergency.

'Well do I remember shooting my first Rhodesian snake,' said Mrs Boggie. She had returned from Gwelo one day to find several of her native employees clustered round a solitary tree, 'herding, to the best of their ability until I should come back, a green mamba up amongst the top-most branches.' This is a species which grows to a length of 9 feet and is one of the most poisonous snakes in Africa: its bite causing death within minutes. Determined to demonstrate that she was capable of using the 'master's big gun', Mrs Boggie loaded both barrels, and, in order to be able to aim directly at the snake's head, which was almost hidden among the green leaves, knelt down on one knee and fired directly upwards.

What a kick that gun did give! It knocked me clean over. Next thing I knew I was lying on my back, and the gun—still loaded in the left barrel and at full cock—was somewhere away over my head.

The snake, however, was dead. After tea, Mrs Boggie insisted that we played a game (involving throwing up and catching little stones), which she herself had played as a child. She possessed a number of cats, mostly elderly, one of which was made to perform its party piece of jumping over her linked hands as she bent down, even though the poor animal seemed well past any such strenuous activity.

An aeroplane passed overhead, and Mrs Boggie frowned. Whereas I enjoyed watching it, she took a completely different view. When, in 1953, it had been announced that training at Thornhill air base would cease the following year, she was relieved that she would now 'get relief from that intolerable, unbearable night flying at low level'.³ However, her relief was to be short-lived, for shortly afterwards, a squadron of de Havilland DH.100 'Vampire' jet aircraft were relocated to Thornhill from Salisbury. Said she:

> Soon the jets were screeching and roaring, not much above tree-top level ... over my own homestead, my cattle-kraal and my dip tank. They terrified the milk cows and caused them to kick over the milk boys [i.e. those who performed the milking]. Also, they terrified the trek oxen when being inspanned [harnessed to wagons].

There followed a battle: the authorities, for their part, assuring Mrs Boggie that the jets should 'normally not be below one thousand feet'; she complained bitterly: 'the usual height of the jets when crossing Boggie's Kopje [*koppie*] where my house stands, is 90 ft. They do not rise in height [when they fly] above the Kopje'.⁴

In her book *A Husband and a Farm in Rhodesia*, Mrs Boggie made some interesting remarks about domestic servants in general, and about their offspring in particular:

> [An 'outstanding matter', was] the steady increase of stealing by our African house boys, hen boys, and especially our *piccanins*. I do not remember ever to have had—in recent years—an honest *piccanin*. They slip into one's house to grab the things of the white *inkosakaas* [mistress] when her back is turned. And apropos of stealing by house boys, I no longer keep a house boy. So it must have been a *piccanin*, sweeping up leaves, who stole the heirloom gold watch.... Also my gold good-luck bracelet, both of which were in a cupboard, unfortunately left with the key in the lock. But the working *piccanin* is today, in 1959, almost a thing of the past. These black children now remark proudly: 'We don't work. We go to school'. And when they are finished with school, or during school holidays, even farm *piccanins* look on farm work as quite beneath their dignity.⁵

Finally, Mrs Boggie related an amusing story about her nephew, Charles, who had been sent out from Scotland by his parents to Southern Rhodesia in the 1920s, in the hope that this would 'make a man of him'. Far from it! Instead, Charles idled his time away and squandered the allowance, which his parents sent him, on drink and gambling.

It was Charles's habit, she said, to go off into the bush for days, and sometimes weeks on end, prospecting in the hope of finding the gold or precious stones which would make him his fortune. Once, his pocket watch having stopped, he lit a bonfire on the railway track and stopped the train, in order to ascertain from the driver what day of the week and date of the month it was.

Charles's parents wrote asking if he was prospering, and when he answered in the affirmative they announced to his dismay that they intended to come out and visit him. Consternation! What was to be done? Charles found the solution by persuading a friend to 'lend' him his farm, the fields of which he proceeded to pack with animals 'borrowed' from neighbours. When his parents arrived, Charles impressed them by waving expansively, and telling them that all the land and cattle as far as the eye could see belonged to him. However, the ruse backfired. His parents informed him that, as he was doing so well, he was clearly no longer in need of his allowance, which they proceeded to cancel forthwith.

Thanks to Mrs Boggie and her legacy of the books that she had written, much of Southern Rhodesia's history has been preserved for posterity. As for the lady herself, there was no doubt in our minds that she embodied the spirit of a true pioneer.

20

The Afrikaners

Before we went to Africa, I had never met a Dutchman, let alone an Afrikaner (Central or Southern African of Dutch descent), yet here they were aplenty, with accents at which to marvel and names with which to conjure: Cornelius Esterhuisen, Frik du Plessis, Maree Coetzee, Elsie Dippenaar, and Ernie du Toit.

In the main, my Afrikaner schoolfellows were pleasant and easy going. Some, however, showed a definite anti-British bias, which manifested itself in such pettinesses as failing to give a pass to a non-Afrikaner on the rugby field if another Afrikaner was to hand, and talking in disparaging terms about anything British. A rare exception to this rule occurred when an enormous delta-winged Avro Vulcan bomber of the UK's RAF flew overhead, and the Afrikaners grudgingly admitted that in aviation, at least, Britain led the world. There was also a degree of bullying, and a disapproving reaction to anyone who referred to Britain, and particularly to England, as 'home'.

One day, I asked one of my Afrikaner classmates, the son of a farmer, why he felt so bitter. The reason, he said, was because of the treatment (or in his view the maltreatment) of his people during the Boer Wars. He spoke of women and children being herded into 'concentration camps' where noxious substances were added to their food deliberately, including ground glass in order to give them bloody diarrhoea.

The seeds of this conflict went back many years. Colonisation of the Cape of Good Hope by the Dutch began in earnest with the Dutch East India Company's establishment of a charter, granted in The Hague on 20 March 1602. The first Dutchman to settle in the Cape was the surgeon Jan van Riebeek (born in Holland in 1619) in 1652—the first Dutch settlers arriving there shortly afterwards. Although Dutch persisted as the written and cultural language until the nineteenth century, the Dutch settlers developed their own language, Afrikaans, which evolved during the Dutch East India Company's 150-year occupation of the Cape. The British presence dated from the time of the Napoleonic Wars, when the Cape was seized from the Dutch—the first British settlers arriving in 1806.

In 1833, the British House of Commons passed a law forbidding slavery throughout the dominions of King William IV. At that time, there were in excess of 30,000 slaves in the Cape Colony and it was upon them that the farmers, who were mainly Boers, depended for their economic survival. Compensation was offered, but it was deemed to be inadequate. This, together with a dislike of bureaucracy and taxation, was the main reason for the Boers taking the decision to leave the Cape Province.

In 1836, the Boers began a 'Great Trek' eastwards, where, after many a bloody battle with the indigenous Zulus, they established the Republic of Natal. However, in 1843, when Natal was officially declared to be a British province, the Boers were forced to make further treks into what became the Transvaal and the Orange Free State, which, in the same year, were declared Independent Boer Republics.

The first Boer War (1880–81) arose with an attempt by the Boers of the Transvaal to assert their independence. This culminated with a defeat for the British at Majuba (the 'Hill of Doves') near Charlestown on the border with Natal. With the discovery of gold in the Transvaal, people of many nations had flocked to that area in the hope of making their fortunes. However, they were not welcomed by the Boers under their president, Paulus Kruger, who referred to them as '*Uitlanders*' (immigrants).

In 1890, Cecil Rhodes became Prime Minister of the Cape Colony. In 1896, however, he was to make a gross error of judgement over a matter concerning the Boers. Taking the side of the *Uitlanders*, and also hopeful of unseating President Kruger, he leant his support to an invasion of the Transvaal, to be led by his close friend Dr Jameson. Yet the so-called 'Jameson Raid' of January 1896, which was seen by the Boers as an attempt by Britain to get her hands on the mineral riches of the Transvaal, ended in failure. Its leaders were imprisoned by the Boers (though treated humanely and later released), and Jameson was sent back to England where he was tried and sentenced to fifteen months' imprisonment. Severely criticised for his support of the abortive Jameson Raid, Rhodes was forced to resign as Prime Minister of the Cape and temporarily to relinquish his position as Managing Director of the BSAC.

In the Second Boer War (1899–1902), the Boers began by invading Natal and Bechuanaland from their Republics of Transvaal and Orange Free State. Initially, they met with great success, and in the so-called 'Black Week', between 10 December and 15 December 1899, Britain suffered three major defeats—at Stormberg, Magersfontein, and Colenso. Boer penetration, deep into Cape Province, then enabled them to besiege Kimberley and also Mafeking in Bechuanaland (in fact, at the commencement of hostilities, Rhodes was visiting Kimberley, where he remained throughout its 124-day siege by the Boers).

General Sir Redvers Buller was now replaced by Lord Roberts as Commander-in-chief of British Forces, with Lord Kitchener as his chief of staff. Having been considerably reinforced, Roberts, on 7 February 1900, transformed the situation by bringing about the surrender of the Boer General Piet Cronje at Paardeberg, 30 miles east of Kimberley on the Modder river. A fortnight later, Bloemfontein, capital of the Orange Free State, fell to the British, who, on 27 May, crossed the Vaal river at Vereeniging, and on 5 June captured Pretoria, capital of the Transvaal.

However, the Boers under their supreme commander, General Louis Botha, refused to surrender and a guerrilla war began in which they, at first, achieved some success. To combat this, the British operated a 'scorched earth' policy. Boer homesteads and farms were burnt down in order to prevent their occupants aiding the Boer men-folk; the families being left to fend for themselves in the open air.

In 1900, Kitchener replaced Roberts as Commander-in-Chief. His tactics were systematically to cordon off vast tracts of land in order to drive the Boer guerrillas into a confined space, while at the same time interning tens of thousands of Boer women and children in so-called 'concentration camps' (still talked about with great bitterness by the Afrikaners at my school, as already mentioned). By separating the menfolk from their homes and families, it was hoped that the Boer guerrillas would lose heart and give in (which, finally, they did). In accordance with Lord Kitchener's policy, a total of forty-five tented encampments were built for Boer internees (and sixty-four for black Africans). Were these camps simply places of internment, or was there unnecessary brutality shown? This will be discussed shortly. Some 28,000 Boer males were captured. Virtually all were sent into exile oversees, to such places as India and Bermuda; those remaining behind were mainly women and children.

Emily Hobhouse, from Cornwall, England, daughter of an Anglican rector, made strenuous efforts on behalf of the Boer prisoners. Said she:

Emily Hobhouse. (*Photo: Collection of the Anglo-Boer War Museum, Bloemfontein, South Africa*)

It was late in the summer of 1900 that I first learnt of the hundreds of Boer women who became impoverished, and were left ragged by our military operations.... The poor women who were being driven from pillar to post, needed protection and organized assistance.

Having created the South African Women and Children's Distress Fund, she sailed for South Africa on 7 December 1900.

Emily was granted permission to take a railway wagon, loaded with supplies, to the Bloemfontein (capital of the Orange Free State) camp, where her worst fears were realised. She said:

[The internees] went to sleep without any provision having been made for them, and without anything to eat or drink. I saw crowds of them along railway lines in bitterly cold weather, in pouring rain—hungry, sick, dying and dead. Soap was an article that was not dispensed. The water supply was inadequate. No bedstead or mattress was procurable. Fuel was scarce and had to be collected from the green bushes on the slopes of the kopjes [*koppies*] by the people themselves. The rations were extremely meagre, and when, as I frequently experienced, the actual quantity dispensed fell short of the amount prescribed, it simply meant famine.

In a side swipe at the British authorities who ran the camp, she declared that she was unable to forgive what she termed 'crass male ignorance, helplessness and muddling'. The attitude of the military was, she said, that 'the whole thing is a grievous and gigantic blunder and present[s] almost insoluble problems, and they don't know how to face it...'[1]

Emily visited several other prison camps in the Orange Free State. In the camps, relatives of those Boers who had failed to surrender to the British were placed on the lowest ration, which, being insufficient to support life, almost invariably ended in starvation and death. Lizzie van Zyl, for example, one of the children whom Emily Hobhouse visited, suffered this fate. Another child victim, Abraham Carl Wessels, was more fortunate in that he survived. Emily also observed that diseases such as measles, bronchitis, pneumonia, dysentery, and typhoid had pervaded the camp, often with fatal results.

Emily subsequently produced a fifteen-page report, which she circulated to the British Government's MPs. This led to the creation of the Government's Fawcett Commission, which suggested many improvements. As a result of Emily's exertions on behalf of the Boers, the death rate in the camps fell from 34.4 per cent in October 1901 to 6.9 per cent in February 1902, and it continued to fall even further from then onwards. The Boer War finally ended in May 1902.

As a mark of the love and esteem that the Afrikaner nation felt towards Emily Hobhouse, and learning that her financial position was precarious, they subsequently raised the sum of £2,300 in order that she might purchase a house for herself on England's Cornish coast—Cornwall being her home county. She died in London in 1926. Her ashes were taken to Bloemfontein to be interred beneath the Women's Monument.

My Afrikaner school friends had voiced the opinion that noxious substances had deliberately been introduced into the food given to the inmates of the British concentration camps. Was this true? Said Johan van Zyl, museum researcher at the Anglo-Boer Museum, Bloemfontein:

> We, at the museum, have not come across any reported cases of poison that happened in the Boer War concentration camps. The camp inhabitants were ill-treated in many a way, but no proof was found that people died of poisons.

Van Zyl did point out that fishhooks had been found in their meat rations. However, some of this bully beef had been canned in the US, at factories where Irish people were employed. It was therefore possible that they had introduced fishhooks into the food in the hope that it might be given to British soldiers.

The question of whether sugar had been deliberately contaminated with ground glass was answered in 1901, when Dr Pratt Yule, Medical Officer of the Orange River Colony, sent a random sample of sugar, supplied to the camps by Champion & Co., a local firm, to the South African Chemical and Metallurgical Laboratory for analysis. This followed complaints about the poor quality of the sugar, and in particular the presence of blue crystals in it. Dr Yule received the laboratory report, compiled by Dr P. D. Hahn, on 26 September 1901. It read as follows:

> It was very impure, containing a rather large amount of fibrous material derived from straws and bags. The sugar contains only an unusually large amount of ultramarine [noted to be present in the form of blue crystals] but no irritants. Ultramarine as such is quite harmless, but should not be contained in pure white sugar. The object of adding ultramarine to sugar is the removal of the yellowish colour of the less refined kinds of sugar, blue being the complimentary colour to yellowish tints.

According to Elris Wessels, Senior Historian at the Anglo-Boer Museum, the sugar crystals were very large, hard, and of irregular size, such that at first glance they could be mistaken for fragments of glass.[2]

The treatment by the British of Boer prisoners in the camps was therefore at best neglectful and incompetent, and at worst cruel and vindictive. This was the reason why my Afrikaner schoolfellows had felt so aggrieved, and justifiably so. Thanks primarily to the work of Emily Hobhouse, the sufferings of the Boer families were made known to the world.

As for the Afrikaners of the 1950s, the old animosities towards the British were part of their folklore, which had been handed down from father to son over several generations. In this respect, they lived in the past and were seemingly oblivious to the possibility of a future in which, sooner or later, the anger of Southern Rhodesia's increasingly disillusioned black majority would boil over.

21

The Death of Rhodes: Inyanga

On 26 March 1902 (a little over a year after the death of Queen Victoria), Rhodes himself gave up the long struggle against ill health and died at Muizenburg, Cape Province. After lying in state at his Cape Town residence, *Groote Schuur* (literally, the 'Great Barn'—which had been converted into a house and was purchased by Rhodes in 1891), and at Parliament House in Cape Town, his coffin 'was placed in a special train, draped in black and purple for the long journey to Bulawayo':

When the train reached Kimberley, 15,000 mourners filed past the open windows to pay their last respects, among them the son of Lobengula, whose education had been paid for by Rhodes. As the train steamed slowly on, a thousand Africans were building a road from Rhodes' farm in the Matopos to Malindidzimu (Rhodes' favourite place, which he called 'A View of the World, and where he expressed the wish to be buried). Skilled masons began to hew out the tomb in solid granite, and the 3-tonne granite seal which was to enclose the tomb.

From Bulawayo on April 9, the mule-drawn gun carriage bearing the coffin moved on under mounted police escort to the thatched summerhouse at Rhodes' farm. On the 10th the mules were replaced by twelve black oxen especially trained to draw the weight of the carriage up the steep slope of the great granite dome. As the cortége drew near the hill, thousands of Africans from every corner of Matabeleland rose, and on a signal from their chiefs gave the royal salute, never before accorded to a white man.[1]

The bronze plaque on his tomb bears the simple inscription:

HERE LIE THE
REMAINS OF
CECIL JOHN
RHODES

Under the terms of his will, Rhodes bequeathed not only the major part of his Inyanga estate (in the eastern highland region of Southern Rhodesia, which became known as the 'Rhodes Inyanga National Park) to the nation, but also his Matopos estate near Bulawayo. As for *Groote Schuur*, this became the official residence of successive governors and state presidents of South Africa.

On 31 May 1902, the peace treaty was signed at Pretoria, bringing the Boer War to an end. British casualties totalled 97,477, of which 5,774 were killed (with more than three times that number dying from wounds, accidents, or disease). Boer losses were estimated at 6,000 men killed, not including deaths in the so-called concentration camps.

In 1896, following his first visit to the region, Rhodes had remarked to his Rhodesian agent:

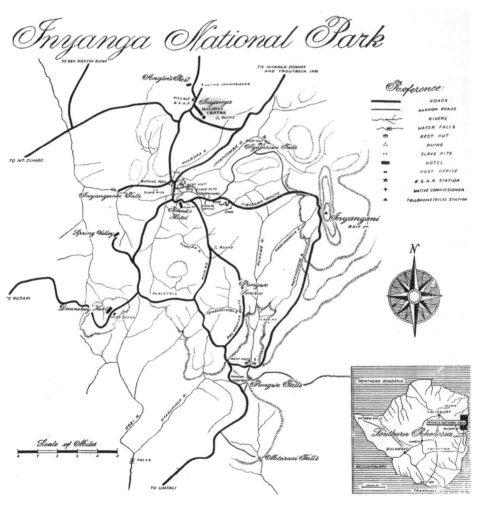

Inyanga National Park.

Inyanga is much finer than you describe. I find a good many farms are becoming occupied. Before it is all gone, buy me quickly up to 100,000 acres and be sure you take in the Pungwe Falls. I would like to try sheep and apple-growing.[2]

The agent did as he was bid, and Rhodes's Inyanga estate became a favourite place—a great deal of his leisure time being spent at Fruit Field Farm, which became his mountain retreat. The following year, Harry Pickstone, a horticulturalist, was brought out from California to plant 150,000 fruit trees, both here and at Rhodes's Matopos estate.[3]

To travel in Inyanga (the word meaning literally 'witch doctor' or 'divine'), as we discovered for ourselves, is to enter another world; one of lush greenery—the annual rainfall here being four times the national average on account of moist air being blown in from the Indian Ocean across Mozambique (the resultant cloudiness of the sky being referred to as a '*guti*').

Here is a landscape of rolling moors, rich in ericas, proteas, aloes, and everlastings; interrupted frequently by ancient, brooding granite hills, mountains, and ruins rich in legend. Embroidering the whole scene is a tracery of clear, sparkling trout streams, terminating abruptly in spectacular waterfalls.[4] Here, for the first time since leaving England, we saw oak trees and apple orchards.

The Inyanga Holiday Centre where we stayed belonged to the Rhodesia Holiday Association: a non-profit-making organisation supported by the trustees of the state lottery. Everybody ate in the communal dining hall, and in the evenings, there were organised games such as beetle drives and dancing (for the young, this meant jiving, which was popular in those days).

Our visit was made in January, during the rainy season, when cars often became stuck in the sticky, red mud of the dirt roads. When this happened, friendly black locals would miraculously appear from the bush to render assistance for a '*tickie*' or two (it was the same if anybody had a puncture). On one occasion, however, they failed to materialise. 'There's only one thing for it, I'm afraid dear,' said my father to my mother. 'You'll have to get out and push.' He said this not because he was unchivalrous, but because he simply did not trust my mother at the wheel of the car. Fortunately, she had brought with her a pair of wellington boots, which she donned before making her way gingerly round to the rear of the vehicle. However, just as she was about to push, my father revved the engine and we shot forward; my mother (who happened to be wearing a new skirt with a strawberry pattern, which she had made herself) was covered with mud from head to foot. That was just before she hit the ground.

World's View (not to be confused with the place of the same name in the Matopos), situated just to the north of the National Park, was aptly named. From it, we could see Mount Inyangani (at 8,517 feet, Rhodesia's highest mountain), beyond which was Mozambique; the Vumba Mountains near Umtali; the Mtoko Hills to the north; and the mountains of Mlanje and Zomba in Nyasaland, some 200 miles away. As for the flora, the guide book summed up the situation perfectly:

> Although man-made wattle, pine and eucalyptus forests have largely replaced the msasa, mlanje cedar and yellow-wood trees which cling to the eastern slopes of Mount Inyangani, the flowers of the uplands thrive and include flame lilies, the red fire lily, gladioli, ground orchids, heathers and everlastings.[5]

Yes, it was undeniable that the beauty of nature was spread out all around us. In my opinion, however, the flame lily referred to above, with its petals varying from crimson to yellow, and curving up and away from the centre and ending in a point, which was Rhodesia's unofficial floral emblem, was the most beautiful flower of all.

We visited the Inyangombe Falls; there to slide down the waterfall, allowing the current to carry us along until we reached a wire suspended across the river (so positioned as to prevent us from being swept away). It was a relief, for once, to be able to bathe in the mountain pools and streams: these being too cool and too fast-flowing to support the bilharzia parasite. Neither were there crocodiles or hippo in any of Inyanga's waters. Immediately above the Falls was a low-level bridge, reminding us of stories we had heard about how, after the rains, the rivers in this region rise with frightening rapidity, sometimes sweeping cars and other vehicles away and even the bridges themselves.

Throughout the park, we encountered numerous ancient and mysterious stone-lined circular hollows, each about 20 feet in diameter, 6 feet deep, each accessed by way of a tunnel only 2 feet wide. The purpose of these structures has never been satisfactorily explained. One theory is that they were 'slave pits'—holding areas for slaves being transported from the hinterland to the coast. Could Rhodesia's most famous monument, Great Zimbabwe, have also fulfilled such a function?.

Federation

The Federation of the two Rhodesias (Northern and Southern) and Nyasaland had come into being in 1953—three years prior to our arrival in the country. Like most teenage boys I had little interest in politics and no idea about the political manoeuvrings that had preceded its creation. I subsequently learned that the people involved, who included representatives of the increasingly, influential black African majorities in the three countries concerned, were by no means of one accord over the matter, as will now be seen.

Raphael Welensky (knighted in 1953 and known as Sir Roy), a larger-than-life character in every way, was greatly admired by us schoolboys on account of his having become Professional Heavyweight Boxing Champion of Rhodesia when he was only nineteen years of age. Born in 1907 in Salisbury, Southern Rhodesia's capital city, his father was a Jew from Russian-ruled Poland, and his mother was of Afrikaner descent.

Welensky commenced his working life as a fireman on Rhodesia Railways and graduated to engine driver; he married and made his home at Broken Hill in Northern Rhodesia.[1] In 1938, he was elected an unofficial member of the Northern Rhodesia Legislative Council, and in 1941, he co-founded the Northern Rhodesia Labour Party.

In late 1948, on a visit to London as a member of a Northern Rhodesian delegation, Welensky stated that his 'particular concern was to find out what Britain's rulers thought about the prospect of closer association between the three Central African territories of Southern Rhodesia, Northern Rhodesia and Nyasaland'.[2] This, in his view, would be ideal step forward, and for the following reasons:

> Two at least of the three territories had a chance, I was convinced, of achieving greatness, but together and not in isolation. Northern and Southern Rhodesia had complementary economies. Northern Rhodesia possessed its increasingly prosperous copper mining industry; Southern Rhodesia had coal, which that

Sir Roy Welensky and Sir Harold
Macmillan.

industry needed; and across the border from Northern Rhodesia was the then rich
and well-ordered Belgian Congo, which also needed coal. Southern Rhodesia was
producing a growing range of consumer goods for which Northern Rhodesia was
an expanding market. The two territories already possessed a common currency,
common meteorological services and a single railway system. [Furthermore] An
apparatus for making co-operation closer already existed in the Central African
Council, which had had a permanent secretariat in Salisbury for the past 3 years.[3]

However, when Welensky suggested to the Secretary of State for the Colonies, the
Right Honourable Arthur Creech-Jones (Labour), an amalgamation of Southern
and Northern Rhodesia, he was met with a flat refusal:

Do you really believe, Mr Welensky, that any government, either Tory or Socialist,
would ever consider either granting Northern Rhodesia a constitution like Southern
Rhodesia's, or if there were amalgamation of the two, the kind of constitution
which would place the control of several million black people in the hands of a few
hundred thousand Whites? No government, irrespective of its political hue, would
carry out that kind of action today. The world wouldn't put up with it.[4]

Instead, said Welensky, Creech–Jones made this suggestion to him:

> Why didn't I turn my thoughts in the direction of some kind of federal system of government? Would this not establish the economic strength and political stability which I was so anxious to achieve in Central Africa, and at the same time give the territories that were part of it rights which could not be eroded?[5]

The fact that, at this juncture, Nyasaland had not entered into the equation did not greatly perturb Welensky, who took the view that 'its contribution towards a federation would consist of little more than its manpower, its tea, tung (a tree producing oil-containing seeds), and one or two other commodities, and that economically it would from the outset be more of a liability than an asset'.[6]

Finally, on 16 February 1949, a conference took place at Victoria Falls in order 'to consider the possibilities of a form of federal association between the three territories'.

Two vital ingredients, however, were missing: no representative from the British government was present and no black African had been invited. This was despite the fact that Welensky had asked Godfrey Huggins, Prime Minister of Southern Rhodesia (since 1933), 'if it might be possible to invite an African representative from Southern Rhodesia'—a suggestion that Huggins declined.[7]

Sir Stewart Gore Browne, who had represented African interests in the Northern Rhodesian Legislative Council since 1938, apprised the conference of the fears of the Africans in Northern Rhodesia and Nyasaland, which were fourfold.

> First they were afraid that if there were any closer links with Southern Rhodesia— which was their big bogey—they would lose their land. They were afraid that political progress would be curtailed. They were afraid that there would be an extension to their territories of what they regarded as Southern Rhodesia's rigid and reactionary pass laws. [This was something of an exaggeration, as will be seen.] Finally, they feared that there would be social and educational discrimination against them.[8]

On 24 November 1949, Welensky put to the Northern Rhodesian Legislative Council 'a motion urging the British government to accept the fact that time was opportune for it to take the lead in creating a Central African federal state':

> However, if the United Kingdom government is genuine in their desire to see the African progress, then they must recognize that one of the fundamentals for that progression is the economic development of these territories. Political rights, after all, mean very little to a man with an empty stomach. If we are genuinely concerned about the Africans let us give them economic development, and political rights can come later. That is secondary consideration.[9]

On 5 March 1951, a conference of officials from the Commonwealth Relations Office, the three territorial governments, and the Central African Council was held in London. The African National Congress (ANC, one of whose avowed aims was universal suffrage), however, made it perfectly clear that it was 'completely opposed to any form of federation, amalgamation or association with Southern Rhodesia, on the now very familiar grounds of fear of a less liberal attitude towards the African population'.[10]

On 13 June 1951, the report of the conference was published: it was unanimous in recommending that a federal system be adopted. Welensky, however, declared that he and Huggins 'were gravely concerned at the break-neck speed with which the British government wanted to hand over control to the Africans'. Instead, what was needed was a step by step approach 'at the rate of which the African showed himself capable of'.[11]

Dr Hastings Banda of the Nyasaland ANC was the person least enamoured of the idea of federation. Having worked in various capacities in Southern Rhodesia and South Africa, he was sponsored to travel and study in the USA, where, in 1931, he graduated in history and political sciences, and in 1937, qualified as a doctor. In 1938, he moved to Edinburgh, Scotland, where, having fulfilled British requirements for medical registration, he entered into general practice: first in the north of England and then in the London suburb of Harlesden. With the founding of the Nyasaland African Congress in 1944, Banda took an increasingly active interest in African politics—attending the Pan-African Congress of 1945 held in Manchester, where he met Kwame Nkrumah of the Gold Coast.

On 7 March 1952, Banda, now the London representative of the Nyasaland ANC, addressed a public meeting in Edinburgh called by the World Church Group. A motion was adopted, demanding that no scheme for closer association of the Rhodesias and Nyasaland 'should be imposed without the free consent of the African peoples'.[12]

At another conference, held in London on 23 April 1952, provision was made for black persons to be included as members: two in the Southern Rhodesian delegation (one being Mr Joshua Nkomo, about whom more will be said later) and two in that of Northern Rhodesia, and also for a black delegation from Nyasaland. In the event, however, the black representatives from Northern Rhodesia and Nyasaland failed to attend the meeting, but agreed to join informal talks in which they reaffirmed 'their unanimous opposition to federation'.[13]

A final conference was held in London on New Year's Day 1953.[14] During the month of discussions (said Welensky), the barrage of hostile propaganda was incessant. Dr Banda and Mr Michael Scott (the Reverend Michael Scott of the Africa Bureau) organised the arrival in the UK, by air, of five tribal chiefs from Nyasaland. They addressed meetings in London, Edinburgh, Birmingham, Manchester, and Glasgow, and told the *Daily Herald* newspaper that they would address an appeal against federation to their 'Great Mother the Queen'.

The report of the London Conference (which was published as a White Paper) stated as follows:

> Southern Rhodesia would continue to enjoy responsible internal self-government in accordance with its constitution. Northern Rhodesia and Nyasaland would remain under the special protection of the Crown. Eventually, it was hoped, the Federation would attain full membership of the Commonwealth.[15] [British Commonwealth of Nations, established 1931.]

The Federation of Rhodesia and Nyasaland was formally inaugurated on 3 September 1953, with British Army officer and politician Lord Llewellyn as Governor-General. Sir Godfrey Huggins became Prime Minister of the Federation's interim government, with Welensky as Minister for Transport, Communications and Post, whereupon Garfield Todd, a New Zealander who had been a missionary in the Shabani area of Southern Rhodesia for some years, succeeded Huggins and became Prime Minister of Southern Rhodesia. In Northern Rhodesia, the number of African members on the Legislative Council was increased from two to four (out of a total of twenty-six in all). Meanwhile, Dr Banda of Nyasaland, who had opposed the idea of federation from the very beginning, relocated to the Gold Coast where he set up in medical practice in the northern provincial city of Kumasi. The move was undoubtedly inspired by that country's visionary and revolutionary leader Kwame Nkrumah, who, in Welensky's words, 'was eager to fulfil his Pan-African dreams as quickly as possible'.[16]

Despite the name 'Federation', there was some variation in the degree of autonomy allowed to the three provinces. Nyasaland, which was the least developed, was ruled by Britain as a crown colony; Northern Rhodesia (despite having its own local assembly and legislative council of elected members) was also governed through the Colonial Office in London; and Southern Rhodesia, which was the most developed, was self-governing and had been so since 1923. However, matters of common concern to all three countries were presided over by the Federal Parliament in Salisbury.

As white schoolchildren, we were encouraged to be proud of the Federation with its coat-of-arms and inspiring motto in Latin: '*Magni Esse Mereamur*' ('Let us Deserve to be Great'). However, not everyone shared this view. One day, I asked Timot for his opinion. He simply shrugged his shoulders, outstretched his hands, palms up, and replied with an expression of utter scorn and disinterest. '*Piccanin baas*, I say to you, what is Federation to me?' His reaction was hardly surprising, bearing in mind that the Federation had been created by the white community whose degree of consultation with the black majority had been only minimal.

23

The Black Population:
Health, Education, Apartheid

Gwelo's hospital for blacks was well appointed and had excellent facilities. However, there were always large numbers of people to be seen waiting outside in its spacious grounds—a reflection of its inability to cope with the proportionately larger black population. It was not uncommon for a would-be patient to walk 10 miles or more in order to be seen. Yet patients diagnosed with leprosy were sent, immediately, to hospital—severe and chronic cases being cared for at the self-contained leper colony at Fort Victoria. However, due to the speed and efficiency with which this disease was treated in the 1950s, it was in decline. For black people, all healthcare was provided free of charge or '*buckshee*', as the locals would say, as was education (with a few exceptions).

Primary education for the black community was provided at government schools (situated either in the townships or in the native reserves), at mission schools, and by local white farmers of their own accord. Such farmers would provide, on their own initiative and at their own expense, a schoolroom furnished with desks and chairs, books, paper and pencils, and, of course, a teacher (on farms that did not possess a schoolroom, lessons would be held out of doors). The offspring of farm workers received their education free of charge. Outsiders, however, could choose either to pay a fee of two shillings and sixpence per week, or work part-time on the farm and be given their schooling *in lieu* of wages.

Secondary education was another matter (there being far more high schools for whites in this category than there were for blacks). However, the Goromonzi High School near the capital Salisbury (the first secondary school for black pupils in Southern Rhodesia), which was opened in 1946, prepared students—as at my own school, Thornhill High—for the Cambridge School Certificate (equivalent to 'Ordinary Level') and for the Higher School Certificate ('Advanced Level'). Now, in the 1950s, another secondary school for black people was proposed near Gwelo. This was the Fletcher High School—the official opening of which took place on 19 April 1958, and to which my family was invited.

The Principal, Staff and Pupils
of Fletcher High School
request the pleasure of the company of

Mr & Mrs Norman

at all the functions connected with
the Official Opening of this School by
Sir Patrick Fletcher, K.B.E., C.M.G., M.P.,
on Friday, 18ᵗʰ of April, 1958,
commencing at 2.15 p.m.

R.S.V.P.
P.O. Box 732, Gwelo.

Invitation to opening of Fletcher High School for Blacks.

First, there was an inter-house football competition, then tea was served, followed by speeches by the Principal Mr W. J. F. Davies, the Director of Native Education, and Sir Patrick Bisset Fletcher, MP and Minister of Lands, Irrigation and Surveys (after whom the school was named). The school was well equipped with library, classrooms (including laboratories and art and woodwork rooms), assembly hall, dining hall, dormitories for the boarders, and a sick bay. The pupils were drawn from the upper echelons of black society: predominantly the sons and daughters of chiefs and tribal elders. They were immaculately turned out in their smart school blazers.

The highlight of the day was an evening performance by the pupils of William Shakespeare's *A Midsummer Night's Dream*, held in the school's open-air theatre—a large grass-covered arena with two tiers of seats, sheltered by a thatched roof. In the refreshingly cool night air, under a sky lit up with a panoply of bright stars as only the African sky can be, the atmosphere was electric. For those who were privileged enough to hear the words of Shakespeare being spoken so nobly by the pupils in their clear, modulated tones, this was an almost supernatural experience. Finally, after a vote of thanks, the pupils sang the movingly beautiful song 'Ishe Komborera Afrika'—'God Bless Africa'. This was followed by the loyal toast to Her Majesty Queen Elizabeth II.

Mr Davies later acquainted my father of the tremendous lengths to which the black pupils were prepared to go in order to acquire knowledge, which had been a revelation to him. For example, when he, the Principal, discovered that the answers of one pupil to examination questions on Shakespeare's *Hamlet* were almost identical to those of another, who was considered to be more able, he suspected that copying had taken place. However, when challenged, the suspect had the last laugh by proceeding to recite, verbatim, the complete play—or, to be more precise, a substantial portion of the first act, after which Mr Davis raised his hands in submission and told him he need go no further.

The multi-ethnic University College of Rhodesia and Nyasaland, which awarded London University degrees, opened at Mount Pleasant, Salisbury, in March 1957. As someone who aspired to be a doctor one day, I was interested to see that at its medical school students were 'taught medical sociology in their second year, to prepare them for dealing with African patients':

It is the only medical school in Africa offering such a course. Studies include Shona clans, totems and philosophy, ancestral worship, spirit possession, propitiation of deceased ancestors, dealings with ngangas and witches, and the kinship marriage and maternity customs of Coloureds, Europeans and Indians.[1]

As for the nurses, they were trained at the newly built hospital for blacks in Salisbury, which offered a full, state-registered qualification. Finally, having completed the three-year course, they would take up appointments in the many hundreds of clinics for blacks, which were situated out in the bush.

The policy of racial segregation of white from non-white, known as 'Apartheid' (an Afrikaans word meaning 'separateness'), had been officially sanctioned in South Africa since 1924, when James Hertzog became prime minister. From 1948, when the National Party came to power in that country under Prime Minister Daniel Malan, it became the official policy of the government. From this time forward, 'Apartheid' legislation in South Africa came thick and fast; the policy being continued by Malan's successors: Johannes Strijdom, 1954–58, and Hendrik Verwoerd, 1958–66.

The Prohibition of Mixed Marriages Act (1959) prohibited marriages between white people and those of other races. The Immorality Amendment Act (1950) prohibited adultery, attempted adultery, or related immoral acts between whites and blacks. The Population Registration Act (1950) led to the creation of a national register in which every person's race was recorded. The Group Areas Act (1950) designated separate residential areas for each race. The Bantu Building Workers' Act (1951) made it a criminal offence for a black person to perform any skilled work in urban areas unless those areas were specifically designated for black occupation.

The Separate Representation of Voters' Act (1951) led to the removal of coloureds (people of mixed race) from the Common Voters' Roll. The Prevention of Illegal Squatting Act (1951) gave the Minister of Native Affairs the power to remove black persons from publicly or privately-owned land. The Native Laws Amendment Act (1952) narrowed the definition of the category of black persons who had the right of permanent residence in towns.

Most detested of all was the Natives Act (1952)—commonly known as the Pass Laws—by which black people were forced to carry identification with them at all times. No black person could leave a rural area for an urban one without a permit from the local authorities. Even if such a permit was granted, work within the urban area had to be obtained within twenty-four hours.

The Native Labour Act (1953) prohibited strike action by black people. The Bantu Education Act (1953), of which Dr Hendrik Verwoerd (then the Minister of Native Affairs, later Prime Minister) was the author, established a black education department in the Department of Native Affairs in order to create a curriculum that suited the 'nature and requirements of the black people'. In other words, the level of education provided was insufficient to enable black persons to qualify for the professions, with the exception of teaching.

The Reservation of Separate Amenities Act (1953) enforced segregation in all public buildings and on public transport. The Extension of University Act (1959) abolished the rights of black students to attend white universities. The Promotion of Bantu Self-Government Act (1959) classified black people into eight ethnic groups—each with its own commissioner general, who was tasked with creating a homeland for each group which would be permitted to govern itself independently, without white intervention. With this veritable plethora of legislation, it was hoped that any possibility of meaningful interaction between blacks and whites would be prevented.

What of Southern Rhodesia, where a policy similar to Apartheid (but known as the 'colour bar') had been in operation since 1933 when Godfrey Huggins had become prime minister? Here, the regime was less strictly enforced than in the Union of South Africa. There were no Pass Laws as such, and the word 'Apartheid' was seldom, if ever, used. Southern Rhodesia's more relaxed and less repressive environment led visitors from the Union of South Africa to remark upon how the whole atmosphere seemed to lighten once they entered the country. Nonetheless, it was advisable for black industrial or farmworkers going on leave to request a form from their employers, stating the latter's name and address. This was to avoid complications should they be stopped by the police for any reason. Additionally, black persons were required to be off the streets of Salisbury by 9 p.m.

As for new white arrivals into the country, such as ourselves, it was made clear that whereas friendliness towards the black community was to be encouraged, fraternisation was absolutely out of the question. The newcomer was expected to adopt the same practices as the local white people, who would not have considered entertaining a black person in their home or taking him or her for a ride in their car (except in an emergency). However, in certain circumstances, close contact between blacks and whites was inevitable as, for example, in the kitchen of Glengarry School. This was presided over by the formidable Mrs Billet (of English origin), who was not averse to chasing Chiguba, the black chef—commonly known as 'Jack'—with one of her kitchen knives if she felt he had been neglecting his duties. When angry, her faced turned to a puce colour, and she hissed like a pressure cooker about to explode. 'Jesus Christ is watching you!' she would yell, pointing the knife heavenwards, whereupon Jack would run for his life, his emotions finely balanced between terror on the one hand and hysterical laughter on the other. Once Mrs Billett had calmed down, peace reigned again and all was forgotten.

There is no doubt that Jack led a precarious existence, and in my opinion, he deserved to be paid danger money for working with Mrs Billett. However, when the chef went down with an attack of bronchitis—through excessive smoking—she came to the rescue by pouring Virol (a sticky, malted restorative), together with nutritious broths, down his throat with a large, wooden spoon, and administering Friar's Balsam inhalations until, like it or not, he recovered. However, as soon as he set foot inside the kitchen again, it was business as usual, and 'where have you put the colander, you stupid kaffir!'

My mother, the school's matron, suggested to Mrs Billet that she might like to make a plum pudding for the pupils' supper. 'Do you have any plums?' she enquired. 'Yes, matron, we have no plums,' came the reply, and from then on, this expression became a standing joke in our family.

In Gwelo, as elsewhere in Southern Rhodesia, it was taken for granted that amenities such as the library, swimming pool, department stores, hospital (the black people had their own), post office, municipal buildings and so forth were for the use of whites only. As for the trains, whites could choose to travel either '1st Class' or '2nd Class', whereas blacks travelled '3rd Class'. As for the buses, whites simply did not use them.

On a visit to the town's swimming pool one day, I experienced the colour bar at first hand. I was sitting at the edge, watching Jane and her friends jumping in off the diving board, when another visitor, an adult male, approached my mother and said angrily, 'Just look at that kid's back. They should be more careful who they let in here!' With horror, my mother realised that the 'kid' to whom the man was referring was me. I had spent so much time out of doors and acquired such a deep sun tan that he had mistaken me for a 'coloured'. 'We can't be putting up with this,' he continued. 'I shall go and speak to the attendant at once!' 'But that is my son!' cried my mother plaintively, whereupon there was an immediate retraction and a profuse apology.

24

The Land Issue:
The Rise of African Nationalism

Although many Shona and Ndebele regarded white people as invaders of their land (despite the fact that they too had arrived from elsewhere, and in doing so had displaced the indigenous population—namely the Bushmen), perhaps their greatest grievance was over the question of the ownership of the land.

Although the system of Apartheid/Colour Bar is regarded as a modern phenomenon, it had its roots in an act of parliament, introduced by Cecil Rhodes in 1894 and known as The Native Reserves Order in Council. The first Native Reserve created by Rhodes was at 'Glen Grey' in a region of the Cape known as Kaffraria. 'My idea,' he said, 'is that the natives should be kept in these reserves and not mixed with white men at all.'[1] He can therefore be justifiably described as being the original architect of Apartheid.

Within the Glen Grey reserve, each black man received an 8-acre allotment on which he was expected to produce enough food for himself and his family. As this was seldom possible, he was therefore obliged to sell his labour outside the reserve to a white farmer or industrialist. Should he fail to do so within a twelve-month period, he would be liable to pay a 'labour tax' in addition to the 'hut tax' payable by every family.[2] The black people had no voting rights outside the reserve, but were permitted to elect 'native councillors' within it.[3] Finally, they were forbidden to sell their land, even if they so wished.

Of the missionaries who ran schools and farms in the Glen Grey area of Cape Province in the late nineteenth century, Rhodes took a dim view. He told the South African Parliament that the 'Kaffir parsons' (native clergy) whom the missionaries were producing, were 'a dangerous class ... [who] would develop into agitators against the government'. He, therefore, proposed to replace the mission schools with industrial schools 'framed by the government' (i.e. where black persons would be taught labouring skills.)[4]

In respect not only of 'the natives in the Colony' (i.e. the Cape), but also 'half a million of natives' on this (the south) side of the Zambesi, and 'another half million on the other side', Rhodes told his members of parliament 'The whole of the North will sometime or other come under this bill if [it is] passed in the House.... This is a native bill for Africa'. In other words, this was to be the blueprint for the establishment of native reserves throughout the whole of British ruled Southern and Central Africa.[5]

By the year 1914 (when the total population of Rhodesia's blacks was about 836,000 and whites 28,000), the land had been apportioned (in million of acres) as follows:

British South Africa Company (BSAC)	48
Blacks	24
Individual White Settlers	13
Private Companies	9[6]

In practical terms, this meant that 3 per cent of the population (white) was in possession of 75 per cent of the land, while the remaining 97 per cent (black) was confined to 23 per cent—i.e. the native reserves. Furthermore, land assigned to blacks was of inferior quality.

In 1914, a commission was set up to investigate growing tensions caused by the conflicting interests of the BSAC and the settlers. However, before the problems could be addressed, war broke out in Europe and white Rhodesians (mainly British) took up arms to support the mother country. In fact, no less than one quarter of the total European population of the country was involved (together with one black regiment) in the fight against the Germans in their colonial territories of East and South West Africa, and in Europe.

When the Union of South Africa came into being on 31 May 1910, it was Bulawayo lawyer Charles Coghlan who helped to draw up its constitution, for which he received a knighthood. It was Coghlan's ambition that Rhodesia merge with the Union, but when a referendum was held in Southern Rhodesia in October 1923 (which was the year of expiry of the BSAC's Charter), the settlers voted by 8,774 votes to 5,999 for domestic self-government, and Coghlan, despite his views, became Southern Rhodesia's first prime minister. However, the 1923 Constitution gave Britain a continuing role in determining policy apropos the black population. As for the BSAC, the British Government paid it £3,750,000 pounds in recognition of its thirty-three-year administration of the country, and it was permitted to retain its commercial and mineral rights.

The Land Apportionment Act of 1930 formalised the division of land between blacks and whites (the black population having now grown to 1.1 million and the white to 50,000) as follows (in millions of acres):

Whites	19
Blacks (in designated Native Reserves)	29
Unassigned, or devoted to Forests or National Parks	9
Native Purchase Areas (available for purchase by natives)	8[7]

The Act also stipulated that no black person was entitled to own land in a white area. When Sir Godfrey Huggins became prime minister in 1933, he summarised the position thus:

> The Europeans in this country can be likened to an island in a sea of black, with the artisan and the tradesman forming the shores and the professional classes the highlands in the centre. Is the native to be allowed to erode the shores and gradually attack the highlands?

In 1951 came the Native Land Husbandry Act, which placed restrictions on black smallholders. It was hugely unpopular and was abandoned ten years later.

Living, as we did, in relatively cocooned isolation on the outskirts of Gwelo, and preoccupied with our own day-to-day living, we were hardly aware of the power struggle that was beginning to develop in and around the capital city of Salisbury, 150 miles to the north-east: a struggle that would one day destroy the entire fabric of the country. Nevertheless, following our arrival in Southern Rhodesia in 1956, it became increasingly obvious to me and to my family—to whom our United Kingdom's House of Commons was the 'Mother of Parliaments'—that before long there would inevitably have to be 'one man, one vote' and black majority rule. Kwame Nkrumah's Gold Coast, for example, was about to become the first of Britain's African colonies to achieve independence. The remainder would surely follow.

The British Protectorate of Uganda, for example, was well on the way to achieving internal self-government, without strife. Likewise, in Tanganyika (a United Nations trusteeship governed by Britain), Julius Nyerere and his Tanganyikan African National Union were currently campaigning for independence. In Kenya, there had been great unrest since 1952, when the Mau Mau (Kikuyu secret society) had begun a terrorist campaign to drive white farmers off the land (resulting in the imprisonment of Jomo Kenyatta, leader of the Kenyan African Union by the British the following year). My school friends were convinced that 'Mau Mau' stood for 'Moscow African Union', and rumours spread that the whole continent of Africa would be subject to a communist takeover. These fears were exploited by die-hard whites who wished to hold on to power. In Algeria, a bitter war was being fought between the National Independence Front and the French colonial army. British Prime Minister Harold Macmillan would later refer to 'The Wind of Change' that was 'blowing through this continent'.[8] However, in Mozambique, an overseas province of Portugal on Southern Rhodesia's eastern border, the struggle for independence was still some way off. At the heart of the independence movement was the African National Congress (ANC).

The African National Congress and the Drive for Independence

Pixley Ka Izaka Seme, a member of that renowned race of former warriors, the Zulus, was born in Natal and educated at Columbia University, New York, and at Jesus College, Oxford. At a meeting convened by him at Bloemfontein on 8 January 1912, Seme, now a qualified lawyer, founded the ANC (originally called the South African Native National Congress)—a multiracial political body—in order to campaign for the rights of the black majority. This was at a time when what few rights the black people possessed were being progressively whittled away.

In 1948, when the Nationalist Party took office in the Union of South Africa with Dr D. F. Malan as prime minister, it began to implement a rigid policy of Apartheid with the creation of black independent homelands. In 1950, in response to the passing of the Group Areas Act that segregated blacks from whites, the ANC began a campaign of civil disobedience. This was to no avail for, in 1955, eviction of the black population from areas designated as 'white' began. The white community was entrenching itself more and more deeply, and it was rumoured that a secret organisation of Afrikaners, known as the 'Broederbond', had pledged itself to resist a black takeover to the last.

What of the Federation of Rhodesia and Nyasaland, and of Southern Rhodesia in particular? Although Britain was taking steps to divest herself of her colonies, the process, as seen through the eyes of the black community, was interminably slow, and it was therefore only natural that it should feel aggrieved. Timot, for instance, owned neither land nor property, nor possessions of any value; nor had he any expectation of doing so, under the current white regime. The majority of my school friends, on the other hand, many of whom were third generation Rhodesians, protested vehemently that they would rather die than hand the country over to the blacks.

As time went by it became clear that the Federation, which Roy Welensky had strived so hard to create, was not working out as he had planned.

> Our chief difficulties lay in the two northern territories, in their governments' relations with the Federal Government, and in the increasingly uncooperative attitude of the African leaders—specifically the Congress Parties—in both territories. The whole [British] Colonial Office system makes them [the black people] see the issue as consisting of two opposed policies, black rule and white rule. They naturally prefer to aim for black rule and hope they will experience this, which they regard as the apotheosis of (British) Colonial Office policy. I thought then, and I think now, that much of the responsibility for the Africans' attitude lay with senior Colonial officials, who resented a federal system.[9]

On 24 January 1957, Lord Llewellin died and was succeeded as Governor-General by Lord Dalhousie. In July that year, Welensky was busy with his proposal for extending the franchise and enlarging the Federal Assembly.

> A Constitution Amendment Act approved by Britain later in 1957 gave further evidence of Britain's continued commitment to a white federation. This act increased the federal assembly from thirty-five to fifty-nine members and substantially increased the ability of white voters to select African representatives and to control African political advance.

However, in the words of US Professor of International Relations Larry W. Bowman, the message that this Act conveyed to Southern Rhodesia's black population was a negative one 'that they were to be systematically and indefinitely excluded from any meaningful access to the federal political system'.[10]

The movements for black independence were becoming increasingly better organised. In Southern Rhodesia, for example, black aspirations were embodied by Joshua Nkomo. A schoolteacher (with a degree in economics and social science), Methodist lay preacher, and former Secretary of the Rhodesian African Railway Workers' Union, Nkomo had been Chairman of the country's ANC since 1951 and its president since 1957.

Meanwhile, there were increasing tensions within Southern Rhodesia's white establishment. For example, 1957, the year after our arrival, was not a happy one for Prime Minister R. S. Garfield Todd. Rumours circulated that Todd had engaged in talks with black nationalist leaders without the approval of his colleagues, and matters came to a head when the members of his cabinet resigned, *en masse*, in protest.[11] The following year, Todd was deposed for exhibiting pro-African sympathies and an election brought Sir Edgar Whitehead of the United Federal Party to power.

In Bulawayo in September 1957, the City Youth League and the City's ANC (founded in the 1930s, but which had since lapsed into obscurity) united to form the ANC of Rhodesia under the leadership of Nkomo. People flocked to join the organisation, which began to challenge the decisions of white native commissioners.

The president of the ANC in Northern Rhodesia was Harry Nkumbula, with Kenneth Kaunda as its Secretary General (in 1955, the pair had been imprisoned for two months for distributing 'subversive' literature).

The President-General of Nyasaland's ANC was Dr Hastings Banda, about whom more will be said shortly.

Robert Mugabe: Influence of Kwame Nkrumah of Ghana: Nyasaland, Catalyst for Change

By a curious coincidence, our adoptive home town of Gwelo would feature in the life of Robert Gabriel Mugabe, who would one day play a decisive role in the future of Southern Rhodesia. His story is as follows.

Mugabe, the third of six children, was born on 21 February 1924 at Matibiri village, situated in the Zvimba District of Southern Rhodesia, 50 miles south-west of the country's capital of Salisbury. His father, Gabriel Mugabe Matibiri, was a carpenter at the nearby Kutama Jesuit Mission Station. His mother, Bona, was 'a devout and pious woman who taught the catechism and the Bible'.[1]

Founded by the Frenchman Jean-Baptiste Loubiére in the early twentieth century, Kutama was an offshoot of the Chishawasha Mission, established by Catholic pioneer missionaries in 1892. At Kutama, Mugabe attended primary school. In 1934, when he was aged ten, his father abandoned the family and went to Bulawayo—Southern Rhodesia's second city, 200 miles away—in search of work. The Mugabe family was thereby deprived of its breadwinner. In the same year, Mugabe's eldest brother, Michael, died of an unknown ailment, and at about this time, Mugabe's elder brother, Raphael, died of an enteric infection. In that year, Father Loubiére died and was replaced by Irishman Father Jerome O'Hea.

Although the prime objective of missionaries like O'Hea was to fulfil what they regarded as their sacred duty to save souls for Christ, they also instilled into their young black charges the ideals of freedom and independence. In other words, they felt no particular allegiance to the prevailing white regime, which could never in its wildest dreams envisage anything other than white rule. O'Hea was no exception, and he undoubtedly had a profound influence on the young Mugabe in this respect. Needless to say, the behaviour of the missionaries angered the majority of white settlers who objected to black persons being educated to such a degree as to give them ideas 'above their station'. As already mentioned, what the whites regarded as the malignant influence of the missionaries was nothing new.

Father O'Hea was an ardent advocate of racial equality, including the provision of education for the black community. He put his beliefs into practice when, at his own expense, he added a secondary school—Kutama College, a technical college—and a teacher training college to the existing facilities at Kutama. He also built a hospital to serve the local Zvimba Native Reserve (which previously had no medical provision at whatsoever).

Kutama College, with O'Hea as its first headmaster, was one of the first institutions to offer a high-school education to Rhodesia's black people. Finding Mugabe to be an assiduous pupil, O'Hea enrolled him at the college. Its motto was '*Esse Quam Videri*'—'To Be, Rather Than To Seem'. O'Hea instructed his pupil 'on the catechism and Cartesian logic [and] gave him a feel for Irish legend and revolution, describing the struggle his fellow Irishmen had sustained to attain independence from Britain'.[2]

Despite his father's absence from home, the young Mugabe had an excellent role model in his mother. As for Father O'Hea, he taught his young pupil to t hink for himself—at any rate, as far as politics was concerned—and to question the colonial system.

Having described Mugabe as having 'an exceptional mind and an exceptional heart', O'Hea offered him a place at Kutama Teacher Training College and also awarded him a bursary (there being no prospect of financial support from the boy's family).[3] As for Mugabe, having embraced O'Hea's anti-colonialist doctrine, the next question was whether or not he would also embrace his mentor's Roman Catholicism.

When, in 1941, Mugabe duly qualified as a teacher, he opted to remain at Kutama, there to teach at his former school. In this way, from his salary of £2 per month, he was able to support his mother and surviving three siblings. In 1944, Mugabe's father, Gabriel, returned with three more children, borne to him by another woman. He was now gravely ill and when, shortly afterwards, he died, Mugabe found himself financially responsible for six children instead of the original three, namely his older brother, Donato, and younger sisters, Sabina and Brigette.

The following year, Mugabe left Kutama to become a primary school teacher at the Dadaya New Zealand Churches of Christ Protestant Mission School, Shabani. Its superintendent was missionary R. S. Garfield Todd, who was soon to make his mark in politics. Like Father O'Hea, Todd was a firm believer in full black enfranchisement.

In 1949, Mugabe, now aged twenty-five, won a scholarship to the University (all-black) of Fort Hare in South Africa's Cape Province—described as a 'hotbed of African nationalism'.[4] Here, he came into contact with many black activists: Leopold Takawira (who introduced him to Marxism), Julius Nyerere, Kenneth Kaunda, Herbert Chitepo, Robert Sobukwe, and James Chikerema (who was also from Kutama). Mugabe later described how his 'hatred and revulsion for the [colonial] system started at Fort Hare. I decided I would fight to overthrow it.'[5]

In Mugabe's early life, therefore, Father O'Hea and Garfield Todd had nurtured the seeds of discontent within him, and the black activists of Fort Hare had instilled in him the ideals of revolutionary Marxism. When the time came, would Mugabe choose to fight in a non-violent way, like Mahatma Gandhi, or would he take up arms like the Bolsheviks of 1917? The answer would not be long in coming.

In 1952, Mugabe, having gained his BA degree in history and English literature at Fort Hare, and having also joined the African National Congress (ANC), returned to Southern Rhodesia (as already mentioned, the ANC had been founded as long ago as 1912: an organisation devoted to bringing all Africans together and to championing their rights and freedoms). In that year, he took up a teaching post at the Driefontein Roman Catholic School near Umvuma, 50 miles east of Gwelo. In 1953, he transferred to Highfield Government School, Harare Township, Salisbury, and in 1954 to Mambo Township Government School, Gwelo.

From 1955–1958, Mugabe, who by now had obtained another degree (BEd—this time by correspondence course from the University of South Africa) was employed as a lecturer at the Chalimbana Teacher Training College in Lusaka, Northern Rhodesia. Meanwhile, in March 1957, Dr Hastings Banda of Nyasaland, who was now living in London, visited newly independent Ghana (formerly the Gold Coast), in order to attend that country's Independence Day celebrations.

In 1958, Mugabe relocated for a period of two years to Ghana. Here he taught at Apowa Secondary School, Takoradi in the west of the country, and studied for yet another degree—BAdmin. It was at Takoradi that he met and fell in love with Sarah 'Sally' Francesca Heyfron, daughter of a fellow teacher at the school.

In Ghana, Mugabe met Prime Minister Dr Kwame Nkrumah, who was an inspiration for many black African leaders. With degrees in economics, sociology, theology, philosophy and anthropology, Nkrumah's first publication *Towards Colonial Freedom*—the title of which is self-explanatory—appeared in 1947. In the same year, he became General Secretary of a new nationalist party, the United Gold Coast Convention. In 1948, urban rioting forced Britain to accelerate the Gold Coast's timetable for devolution. In 1949, Nkrumah created the Convention People's Party, whose slogan was 'Self-Government Now'. In 1950, he was imprisoned for inciting a general strike. In the election of February 1951, he was returned as Parliamentary Member for Accra Central. Gold Coast finally achieved independence (the first British African colony to do so) under its new name of Ghana in March 1957, with Nkrumah as prime minister.

Thereafter, at Nkrumah's invitation, educated black persons from other African countries came to Ghana to study, teach, and derive encouragement for their own nationalistic aspirations. Nkrumah 'was determined, in particular, to turn Ghana into a launching pad for African liberation: providing a base from which nationalist leaders from colonial Africa could draw support and encouragement'.[6]

It is not, therefore, surprising that Mugabe was drawn to Ghana and Nkrumah. Just as O'Hea, Todd, and Fort Hare had nurtured his yearnings for independence, so Nkrumah was now able to demonstrate to him, at first hand, how this could be achieved. Mugabe could also see for himself what the end results of the struggle were; for here, in the newly independent Ghana—unlike in Mugabe's own country—

the proverbial 'glass ceiling' that had prevented black persons from achieving their full potential had simply ceased to exist. Here, Mugabe saw blacks being made directors of companies and appointed to the headships of schools and of civil service departments.

During his time in Ghana, Mugabe attended the Kwame Nkrumah Ideological Institute at Winneba in the south of the country, where he was taught the general principles of Marxism.[7] It would not have escaped his notice that in Marxist/ Leninist USSR, power resided largely in the hands of one person—Josef Stalin (1879–1953)—and in communist China, in the hands of Chairman Mao Zedong (1893–1976). Is it conceivable that he sought such dictatorial power for himself? Or would he choose the democratic option?

Meanwhile, on 6 July 1958, Banda returned to Nyasaland where, on 1 August, he was elected President-General of that country's ANC. On 1 December he attended the all—African Peoples' Conference in Ghana's capital, Accra. Shortly afterwards, when Banda was challenged by a journalist as to whether, when he said he would fight the Federation, this meant that he would resort to violence in order to overthrow it, he replied, 'I mean not with violence but one can't exclude that if we are not allowed to get out of it' (i.e. to leave the Federation).[8]

In the Federal General Election of 11 November 1958, Sir Edgar Whitehead's United Federal Party won by an overwhelming majority. Early in 1959, the Nyasaland ANC sent a delegation to London to meet with the Conservative government's Colonial Secretary Alan Lennox-Boyd. Welensky, for his part, was highly suspicious of the British Government. Said he:

> Saying again and again that they had faith in the Federation, that they wanted to uphold it and see it successful, they encouraged and assisted the growth of forces absolutely inimical to it.

Welensky feared, that with the upsurge of African nationalism and the demand for immediate independence throughout the continent, 'a vast power vacuum was being created, which the communists were only too willing to fill'.[9] He was particularly concerned at the unrest that had accompanied Banda's return to Nyasaland, which he attributed to the verbal attacks that the latter and his colleague H. B. Chipembere were making on the Federation. This had led to cars being stoned and to a police station being attacked by rioters. So serious was the situation that on 21 February 1959, Welensky announced:

> Federal troops, including detachments of the 1st Battalion King's African Rifles from Lusaka (Northern Rhodesia) and 120 European personnel of the 1st Battalion The Royal Rhodesian Regiment were being sent by air to Blantyre (Nyasaland) as a precautionary measure, following serious disturbances at three widely separate points: Karonga, Fort Hill and Rumpi.

News of these events percolated down to us in Southern Rhodesia, and the seriousness of them was brought home even more when, on 26 February 1959, its government declared a state of emergency 'on the grounds that there was a reasonable fear that a situation similar to that prevailing in Nyasaland would occur unless immediate steps were taken to prevent it'.

Meanwhile, in Nyasaland, there was further rioting, with six fatal shootings by the security forces. White women and children now began to leave the country by air, and families living in isolated areas were asked by the police to move into Blantyre for their own protection. Finally, on 3 March 1959, the Governor Sir Robert Armitage declared a state of emergency. Shortly before the announcement was made, 100 or more of the Nyasaland ANC's senior officials, including Banda and Chipembere, were detained, placed in Federal Custody, and transported to prisons outside the Protectorate. According to the *Rhodesia Herald*, Banda was taken into custody 'wearing silk pyjamas and a blue dressing gown'. He was imprisoned in our home town of Gwelo—an event that caused an enormous stir among my classmates, many of whom regarded him as something akin to a poisonous reptile.

A vicious circle now developed with the hatred of many whites (including most of my school friends) towards Banda being equalled by the indignation felt by the blacks at the treatment of their countrymen by the whites. In retrospect, I realised that the vehement opposition to Banda on the part of the whites was based upon fear of a black takeover of the entire Federation.

In respect of Northern Rhodesia's General Election, held in March–April 1959, Welensky criticised Kenneth Kaunda, leader of that country's ANC, who, he said 'made one inflammatory speech after another, in spite of the fact that he assiduously professed his belief in non-violence'.[10]

In the same year, a Commission of Inquiry was appointed under the chairmanship of British lawyer Justice Patrick Devlin to investigate and report on the Nyasaland disturbances to the Conservative government of Harold Macmillan. In July, the Commission reported as follows: 'Nyasaland is—no doubt temporarily—a police state, where it is not safe for anyone to express approval of the policies of the African National Congress Party'.

This was not to the liking of Welensky, to whom the inference was obvious. Said he:

> Since Britain—government, parliament and people—was determined to offload the real responsibilities and obligations of a rulership in Central Africa which she would not hand over to us, the Federation was to be her scapegoat.[11]

As relative outsiders, it became increasingly obvious to my parents that the majority of our white Rhodesian friends were burying their heads in the proverbial sand, by failing to recognise the strength of the 'Wind of Change' and the direction in which it was blowing. Fearful of what the future might hold, we therefore made the decision, in the summer of 1959, to leave Southern Rhodesia and return to England.

26

Farewell: Aftermath: Independence

On 18 August 1959, at a special leaving ceremony organised by the black employees of Glengarry School prior to our departure, Kefas, the laundry boy, made a faltering speech and Jerry, the shoemaker boy, did my father the honour of presenting him with a live chicken ('*hookoo*' in Shona), which was little more than skin and bone. This my father accepted graciously before passing it smartly to Brian Flavell, the deputy head.

The school's chef, Jack, handed my father an envelope containing 13 shillings, which the 'boys' had collected for him as a farewell present. In an accompanying letter, they said they all hoped their new master would be as kind to them as he had been. They had all signed it, except for Edius, the kitchen boy, who could not write and therefore simply made his mark. I noticed that when my father had finished reading this letter, his eyes were filled with tears.

Having to leave our faithful Judy behind almost broke my mother's heart (it was either that or putting the animal into quarantine for six months, which we thought would be unfair to one who, like 'Jock of the Bushveld', was used to the freedom of the great outdoors). My mother scoured the land trying to find the dog a good home and finally succeeded. Judy would spend her remaining days on a farm, living mainly out of doors on the veld, where generations before her ancestors had hunted lion.

I knew I would miss my friends, both black and white, and particularly Timot. However, since our arrival in Southern Rhodesia three years previously, it was noticeable that the atmosphere had changed—that the conviviality previously existing between blacks and whites had given way to suspicion and mistrust. Even Timot had become reserved, and I knew that life could never be the same again. For the blacks, the imprisonment of their leaders, Mr Nkomo, Dr Banda, and the Reverend Sithole, and the proscribing of their political organisations was deeply resented. This became a festering sore that would not heal.

The Federation of Rhodesia and Nyasaland was dissolved on 31 December 1963. In that same year, Dr Banda became Prime Minister of Nyasaland: a position in

Dear Sir,

This is to let you know that all my boys and me have made a collection of 13/- We have done this for you our made as a farewell. We are very sorry that you are going away and leave us alone. We do not know whether the new master will be a kind man like you.

I beg to remain Sir

Yours faithfully

Jack

Chef	Chigubu (Jack)	chigubu
Kitchen	Chamundrgwa (Edius)	+ his mark
	Jefireti	Jefiret
	Vengesayi	Vengesaye
Laundry	Manjera	Manjera
	Tichawona	Tichawona
	James	Jima
Dormitories	Office	Office.
	Shoniwa (Johannes)	J oHannesi
Grounds	Kanos	Kanos
Messenger	Munaro (Solomon)	Munara

African staff, Glengarry School,
August 1959.

Letter from Jack to Chris, with accompanying signed list of Glengarry School's employees.

which he continued after the country achieved its independence the following year under a new name—Malawi. In Northern Rhodesia, Kenneth Kaunda became a cabinet minister in 1961, and president when the country became independent in 1964 as the Republic of Zambia. In respect of his political opponents, Kaunda declared:

> We would like an opposition that is non-tribal, non-racial and non-religious. By non-religious of course, I mean one that is not based on any religious grouping. A sweeping victory at any given election is no mandate to legislate against the formation of an opposition.[1]

Sadly, there were other leaders who failed to follow his example.

In 1959, a prison was built on Robben Island, which we sighted once again on our return journey from Southern Rhodesia to England via Cape Town in that same year.

In April 1960, Dr Banda was released from prison. In May, Mugabe returned to Southern Rhodesia from Ghana with Sarah 'Sally' Heyfron, his Ghanaian wife-to-be. He proceeded to take an active role in politics—campaigning for the National Democratic Party (NDP—a reincarnation of the ANC, which had been banned in January 1960). When the NDP was also banned, the nationalists responded by creating ZAPU (Zimbabwe African People's Union), which was itself banned nine months later. On 6 August 1963, a breakaway party, ZANU (the Zimbabwe African

National Union) was created with the Reverend Ndabaninge Sithole as leader and Mugabe (*in absentia*, as he was currently in Dar es Salaam, Tanganyika) as secretary general.

On 13 April 1964, Ian Smith became prime minister of Southern Rhodesia. In August, Mugabe, having returned home, was imprisoned by the white regime under terms of Section 50 of the Law and Order (Maintenance) Act.

On 12 June of that same year, Nelson Mandela, leader of South Africa's African National Congress (ANC), was sentenced to life imprisonment for conspiracy to overthrow the state. He would serve a total of twenty-seven years—the period 13 June 1964 to 31 March 1982 being spent on Robben Island.

In 1964, both Nyasaland and Northern Rhodesia achieved independence within the British Commonwealth: the former on 6 July as Malawi, with Dr Banda as prime minister, and the latter on 24 October as Zambia, with Kenneth Kaunda as president.

What of Southern Rhodesia? On 11 November 1965, Ian Smith made a unilateral declaration of that country's independence from Britain (UDI). By stubbornly ignoring the 'Wind of Change', his action had the effect of setting the country back a decade and a half and precipitating a civil war.

The following year, a guerrilla war was launched against the white regime: Joshua Nkomo's ZAPU forces operating from Zambia, and ZANU's forces from Mozambique. The aircraft of Thornhill airbase, which, as a schoolboy sitting at my desk, I had watched taking off and landing in more peaceful times, were now used by the government against the 'rebels'.

In November 1974, Mugabe was released after spending more than a decade in prison, whereupon he relocated to Mozambique to take charge of the guerrilla campaign. The following year, he was elected President of ZANU.

Ian Smith was finally forced to negotiate: talks culminating in the Lancaster House Conference, held in London between September and December 1979. In the elections to the House of Assembly of February 1980, the following number of seats were gained by the various parties.

Robert Mugabe's ZANU	57
Joshua Nkomo's ZAPU	20
Ian Smith's Rhodesia Front	20
Bishop Abel Muzorewa's United African National Congress party	3

Finally, at midnight on 17 April 1980, the independent Republic of Zimbabwe came into existence, led by Prime Minister Robert Mugabe.

27

Robert Mugabe:
Blood and Tears

There is no intention on our part to use our majority to victimise the minority. We will ensure there is a place for everyone in this country.[1]

These were Mugabe's words, spoken with apparent sincerity, after his party's victory in the 1980 elections. In August the following year, he wrote to white, Bulawayo-based lawyer David Coltart, offering the following assurances:

> As you are no doubt aware, we, in government, intend to establish a non-racial society based on equality—and the promotion of the well-being of all our people in accordance with our socialist principles. It is in this connection that we have adopted the policy of reconciliation whereby our people must put aside the hatreds and animosities of the past and approach the future in a positive and constructive frame of mind and with commitment and dedication to the all-round development of the new Zimbabwe.[2]

However, as Mugabe, Zimbabwe's new leader, proceeded to establish himself as an absolute dictator, and establish a regime underpinned by the apparatus of a brutal police state, it soon became apparent that his people and the world had been deceived. In 1994, he 'came clean' by openly affirming that, in his opinion, 'The one-party state is more in keeping with African tradition. It makes for greater unity for the people. It puts all opinions under one umbrella, whether these opinions are radical or reactionary'.[3]

The outcome was that Mugabe presided over a seemingly endless reign of terror, during which the majority lived in constant fear from the police, the army, or from his ZANU-PF thugs, who employed the tactics of murder, unspeakable torture, and deliberate starvation. The homes of those who opposed him—almost invariably by peaceful means—were bulldozed or burnt to the ground, and millions were displaced or fled the country.

Mugabe's predecessor, Mzilikazi, King of the Matabele and ruler of the Shona people, was known as 'The Monarch of Blood and Tears'. This description may equally well be applied to Zimbabwe's leader, Robert Mugabe.

Epilogue

Looking back on my time in Southern Rhodesia, I have to admit that neither I nor my family had any particular qualms about belonging to such a society as existed in the colonial era, neither did we agonise about its intrinsic unfairness. This came later, but at the time, it seemed only natural to 'go with the flow', as it were.

It seldom occurred to me to ask Timot, whom I regarded as a friend, for his views, and he certainly did not volunteer them, for any black who had the temerity to demand equal rights and 'one man, one vote' would inevitably have been labelled a troublemaker and sacked from his job.

What did I miss most about Southern Rhodesia? The magnificence of the landscape and its unsurpassed flora and fauna, of course, but more than that, its peoples. The black people, with their ceremonial costumes, creative artistry (which included weaving, wood carving, sculpture, and jewellery making), rich diversity of language, traditional singing and dancing, and, perhaps most of all, their humour. The Afrikaners, who had survived against all the odds and whose heritage of Great Trek and great battles was immortalised in their folk songs; my fellow Britons, who transformed little corners of Africa into a 'Little Britain' by creating gardens, cultivating roses, and playing cricket; and finally others from all parts of the world, who added yet more colour to the rich tapestry of Rhodesian life.

Will 'The Lost Jewel of Africa' ever be found again? Perhaps, perhaps not. Even if it is, it has come too late for those untold millions who are victims of Mugabe's holocaust.

Endnotes

Frontispiece

1. Smith, I. D., *Bitter Harvest: The Great Betrayal,* (London, Blake Publishing, 1981), p. 9.

Chapter 4

1. Rhodesian forces had also fought on the Allied side during the First World War.

Chapter 5

1. Edwards, N., *Jumbo Guide to Rhodesia,* (Salisbury, Southern Rhodesia, Wilrey Publications, 1974), p. 37.

Chapter 6

1. www.barbaragoss.net/rhodesiatapestry/gwelo.html.
2. Salt, B., (ed.), Extracts from the *Rhodesia Herald*, p. 55.
3. *Ibid.,* p. 53.
4. *Ibid.,* p. 50.

Chapter 7

1. Human sewage may contain Schistosoma eggs from an infected person. If these eggs enter freshwater lakes, rivers, and streams, they may infect fresh water snails, which cling to vegetation along the water's edge. Within the snails, the eggs develop into larvae that, on maturity, are released by the snails into the water. Here they swim around and may penetrate the skin of anyone in the water with whom they come into contact, such as a swimmer. Within the human body, the larvae mature into adult worms, both male and female, which mate and produce eggs. The worms can damage the liver, kidneys, and spleen, and cause anaemia, and even cancer of the bladder. Finally, these eggs are excreted in the urine and faeces, and thus the life cycle

of the worm is able to repeat itself. The disease was endemic in all Rhodesian lakes and waterways, except for those in the mountainous regions of the country's eastern districts, where the waters are too cold and fast flowing for the worm to survive.

2. The time would soon come when, as Prime Minister of Southern Rhodesia, his exasperation with the British Government would lead him and his Rhodesian Front party to declare the country wholly independent from Britain—with disastrous consequences.

3. Sputnik I, launched by the Soviets on 4 October 1957, was the world's first artificial satellite. It was followed by Sputnik II, launched the following month, and by eight more Sputniks subsequently.

Chapter 8

1. Edwards, N., *Jumbo Guide to Rhodesia*, (Salisbury, Southern Rhodesia, Wilrey Publications, 1974), pp. 123–4.

Chapter 9

1. Edwards, N., *Jumbo Guide to Rhodesia*, (Salisbury, Southern Rhodesia, Wilrey Publications, 1974), p. 168.
2. *Ibid.*, p. 168.
3. *Wankie Game Reserve: Rhodesian National Park, Salisbury*: Government Printer.
4. *Ibid.*, p. 178.
5. Harris, J., *My Memoirs*, Courtesy of Lynette Hodges (also reported in the *Gwelo Times*).
6. Information kindly supplied by the Livingstone Centre, Blantyre.

Chapter 10

1. Bold, J. D., Fanagalo: *Book, Grammar, Dictionary*, (Pretoria, J. L. van Schaik, 1990), pp. 1–2. The multiplicity of dialects among the black community, and the existence of two main languages—English and Afrikaans—among the white, presented certain difficulties in communication. This is where Fanagalo, or 'Kitchen Kaffir' (a hybrid language that has been spoken since the days of the pioneers, with numerous refinements taking place ever since) came to the rescue. It is defined thus:

> ... a very much simplified version of Zulu, Xhosa and related languages, with adaptations of modern terms from English, Dutch and Afrikaans. It probably evolved in the Eastern Cape and Natal, and later Zimbabwe [formerly Southern Rhodesia] during contacts between European settlers and African tribes.... It developed on diamond diggings, gold mines and farms to meet the urgent need for a common language that could easily be acquired ... and then spread in due course to domestic service and other spheres. Migrant labourers continued to take the knowledge of it back to their own territories, and today it is known from the Cape to Central Africa.

Using Fanagalo, scientists from Witwatersrand University and the Chamber of Mines were even able to communicate with the Bushmen of the Kalahari Desert. In fact, so important did the language become that in 1951, a phrase book, *Grammar and Dictionary of Fanagalo* by J. D. Bold, was published.

Chapter 11

1. Rhodesian Schools Exploration Society: Report, Lower Sabi (River) Expedition, September 1958.
2. Boggie, J. M., *First Steps in Civilizing Rhodesia: Being a True Account of the Experiences of the Earliest White Settlers—Men, Women and Children—in Southern and Northern Rhodesia*, (Bulawayo, Kingstons, 1966), pp. 18–19.
3. *Gwelo Times*, 1 September 1958.
4. Rhodesian Schools Exploration Society, *op. cit.*

Chapter 13

1. Edwards, N., *Jumbo Guide to Rhodesia*, (Salisbury, Southern Rhodesia, Wilrey Publications, 1974), p. 64.
2. Klein, K., 1978, Occasional Papers, National Museum of Southern Rhodesia. A4(2): 74-8, in Bednarik, R., 'The Evidence of Paleoart', Lecture No. 3.
3. Rosenthal, E. (editor and compiler), *Encyclopaedia of Southern Africa*, (London, Frederick Warne & Co., 1973) pp. 39, 63.
4. Boggie, J. M., *First Steps in Civilizing Rhodesia: Being a True Account of the Experiences of the Earliest White Settlers—Men, Women and Children—in Southern and Northern Rhodesia*, (Bulawayo, Kingstons, 1966), p. 206.
5. Middleton, J., (ed.), *Encyclopaedia of Africa South of the Sahara*, (New York, C. Scribner's Sons, 1997), p. 430.
6. Boggie, J. M., *op. cit.*, pp. 207, 210.
7. *Ibid.*, pp. 212, 215.
8. Phillips, T., (ed.), *Africa: The Art of the Continent*, (New York, Prestel, 1995), p. 197. Today, four of the original Great Zimbabwean stone birds are in the collection of the Great Zimbabwe museum, and fragments of others are also to be found here and at Rhodes's former residence, *Groote Schuur*.
9. Edwards, N., *op. cit.*, p. 82.
10. Oliver, R., and Fage, J. D., *A Short History of Africa* (6th ed.), (New York, Penguin Books, 1988), pp. 48–9.
11. Middleton, J., (ed.), *op. cit.*, p. 430.

Chapter 14

1. Boggie, J. M., *First Steps in Civilizing Rhodesia: Being a True Account of the Experiences of the Earliest White Settlers—Men, Women and Children—in Southern and Northern Rhodesia*, (Bulawayo, Kingstons, 1966), pp. 4, 11.
2. *Ibid.*, p. 5.
3. *Ibid.*, p. 8.
4. *Ibid.*, p. 173.
5. *Ibid.*, p. 11.
6. *Ibid.*, p. 11.
7. *Ibid.*, p. 17.
8. *Ibid.*, p. 327.
9. *Ibid.*, p. 14.
10. *Ibid.*, pp. 317–8.
11. *Ibid.*, p. 20.
12. *Ibid.*, pp. 21, 23.

13. *Ibid.*, p. 23.
14. *Ibid.*, pp. 27–9.
15. *Ibid.*, p. 44.
16. *Ibid.*, p. 35.

Chapter 16

1. *Victoria Falls: Greatest River Wonder of the World*, Southern Rhodesia Public Relations Department.

Chapter 17

1. Boggie, J. M., *First Steps in Civilizing Rhodesia: Being a True Account of the Experiences of the Earliest White Settlers—Men, Women and Children—in Southern and Northern Rhodesia*, (Bulawayo, Kingstons, 1966), pp. 186–7.
2. *Ibid.*, p. 188.
3. Gale, W. D., *One Man's Vision: The Story of Rhodesia*, (London, Hutchinson, 1935), p. 171.
4. Thomas, A., *Rhodes: The Race for Africa*, (London, Penguin, 1997), p. 350.
5. Meredith, M., *Mugabe: Power and Plunder in Zimbabwe*, (Oxford, Public Affairs, 2002), pp. 112–3.

Chapter 18

1. Boggie, J. M., *First Steps in Civilizing Rhodesia: Being a True Account of the Experiences of the Earliest White Settlers—Men, Women and Children—in Southern and Northern Rhodesia*, (Bulawayo, Kingstons, 1966), p. 46.
2. *Ibid.*, pp. 65–66, 68.
3. *Ibid.*, p. 61.
4. *Ibid.*, p. 69.
5. Salisbury, Southern Rhodesia, *Evening Standard*, 1 September 1958.

Chapter 19

1. Boggie, J. M., *A Husband and a Farm in Rhodesia*, (Gwelo, Catholic Mission Press, 1959), pp. 13, 15.
2. *Ibid.*, pp. 16–17.
3. *Ibid.*, p. 365.
4. *Ibid.*, pp. 366–7.
5. *Ibid.*, pp. 364–5.

Chapter 20

1. Hobhouse, E., *The Brunt of the War and Where it Fell*, (Thornton Cleveleys, Lancashire, Wilding Press, 2011)
2. Information kindly supplied by the Anglo-Boer Museum, Bloemfontein.

Chapter 21

1. Edwards, N., *Jumbo Guide to Rhodesia,* (Salisbury, Southern Rhodesia, Wilrey Publications, 1974), p. 61.
2. *Ibid.*, p. 92.
3. Thomas, A., *Rhodes: The Race for Africa,* (London, Penguin, 1997), p. 350.
4. Edwards, N., *op. cit.*, p. 95.
5. *Ibid.*, p. 95.

Chapter 22

1. Welensky, Sir R., *Welensky's 4,000 Days: The Life and Death of the Federation of Rhodesia and Nyasaland,* (London, Collins, 1964), p. 14.
2. *Ibid.*, p. 21.
3. *Ibid.*, pp. 21–2.
4. *Ibid.*, p. 23.
5. *Ibid.*, p. 24.
6. *Ibid.*, p. 26.
7. *Ibid.*, p. 27.
8. *Ibid.*, p. 28.
9. *Ibid.*, p. 35.
10. *Ibid.*, p. 37.
11. *Ibid.*, pp. 38–9.
12. *Ibid.*, p. 50.
13. *Ibid.*, p. 52.
14. *Ibid.*, p. 59.
15. *Ibid.*, p. 61.
16. *Ibid.*, p. 110.

Chapter 23

1. Edwards, N., *Jumbo Guide to Rhodesia,* (Salisbury, Southern Rhodesia, Wilrey Publications, 1974), pp. 129–130.

Chapter 24

1. Vindex, Reverend F. V., *Cecil Rhodes: His Political Life and Speeches,* (London, Chapman & Hall, 1900), p. 386.
2. Thomas, A., *Rhodes: The Race for Africa,* (London, Penguin, 1997), p. 279.
3. Williams, B., *Cecil Rhodes,* (London, Constable, 1921), p. 381.
4. *Ibid.*, p. 383.
5. Vindex, Reverend F. V., *op. cit.*, pp. 372, 390.
6. Pre-Independence Legislation on Land: www.raceandhistory.com/Zimbabwe/factssheet.html 11.7.2005.
7. *Ibid.*
8. Macmillan, H., Speech to South African Houses of Parliament, Cape Town, 3 February 1960.

9. Welensky, Sir R., *Welensky's 4,000 Days: The Life and Death of the Federation of Rhodesia and Nyasaland,* (London, Collins, 1964), pp. 72–3.
10. Bowman, L. W., *Politics in Rhodesia in an African State,* (Cambridge, Massachusetts, Harvard University Press, 1973), p. 26.
11. Salt, B., (ed.), Extracts from the *Rhodesia Herald*, p. 46.

Chapter 25

1. Meredith, M., *Mugabe: Power and Plunder in Zimbabwe,* (Oxford, Public Affairs, 2002), p. 19.
2. *Ibid.,* p. 21.
3. Blair, D., *Degrees in Violence,* (London, Continuum, 2002), p. 18.
4. *Ibid.,* p. 19.
5. Blake, R., *History of Rhodesia,* (London, Eyre Methuen, 1978), p. 374.
6. Meredith, M., *op. cit.,* p. 24.
7. *Ibid.,* p. 24.
8. Welensky, Sir R., *Welensky's 4,000 Days: The Life and Death of the Federation of Rhodesia and Nyasaland,* pp. 100, 102.
9. *Ibid.,* pp. 109–10.
10. *Ibid.,* p. 134.
11. *Ibid.,* p. 131.

Chapter 26

1. Hall, R., *Kaunda: Founder of Zambia,* (Lusaka, Zambia, Longmans of Zambia, 1964), p. 82.

Chapter 27

1. Meredith, M., *Mugabe: Power and Plunder in Zimbabwe,* (Oxford, Public Affairs, 2002), p. 15.
2. Mugabe to David Coltart, 19 August 1981.
3. Blair, D., *Degrees in Violence,* (London, Continuum, 2002), p. 29.

Bibliography

Blair, D., *Degrees in Violence* (London: Continuum, 2002)

Blake, R., *History of Rhodesia* (London: Eyre Methuen, 1978)

Boggie, J. M., *A Husband and a Farm in Rhodesia* (Gwelo: Catholic Mission Press, 1959)

Boggie, J. M., *First Steps in Civilizing Rhodesia: Being a True Account of the Experiences of the Earliest White Settlers—Men, Women and Children—in Southern and Northern Rhodesia* (Bulawayo: Kingstons, 1966)

Bold, J. D., Fanagalo: *Book, Grammar, Dictionary* (Pretoria: J. L. van Schaik, 1990)

Bowman, L. W., *Politics in Rhodesia in an African State* (Cambridge, Massachusetts: Harvard University Press, 1973)

Daily Mail.

Daily Telegraph.

Edwards, N., *Jumbo Guide to Rhodesia* (Salisbury, Southern Rhodesia: Wilrey Publications, 1974)

Gale, W. D., *One Man's Vision: The Story of Rhodesia* (London: Hutchinson, 1935)

Gwelo Times, The.

Harris, J., *My Memoirs.*

Hobhouse, E., *The Brunt of the War and Where it Fell* (Thornton Cleveleys, Lancashire: Wilding Press, 2011)

Middleton, J., (ed.), *Encyclopaedia of Africa South of the Sahara* (New York: C. Scribner's Sons, 1997)

Meredith, M., *Mugabe: Power and Plunder in Zimbabwe* (Oxford: Public Affairs, 2002)

Nkomo, J., *Nkomo: The Story of My Life* (London: Methuen, 1984)

Oliver, R., and Fage, J. D., *A Short History of Africa* (6th ed.) (New York: Penguin Books, 1988)

Hall, R., *Kaunda: Founder of Zambia* (Lusaka, Zambia: Longmans of Zambia, 1964)

Phillips, T. (ed.), *Africa: The Art of the Continent* (New York: Prestel, 1995)

Rhodesia Herald.

Rosenthal, E. (editor and compiler), *Encyclopaedia of Southern Africa* (London: Frederick Warne & Co., 1973)

Salt, B. (ed.), Extracts from *The Rhodesia Herald.*

Smith, I. D., *Bitter Harvest: The Great Betrayal* (London: Blake Publishing, 1981)

Thomas, A., *Rhodes: The Race for Africa* (London: Penguin, 1997)

Vindex, Reverend F. V., *Cecil Rhodes: His Political Life and Speeches* (London: Chapman & Hall, 1900)

Welensky, Sir R., *Welensky's 4,000 Days: The Life and Death of the Federation of Rhodesia and Nyasaland* (London: Collins, 1964)

Williams, B., *Cecil Rhodes* (London: Constable, 1921)

Index